Second Edition

YOUTH BASKETBALL
SKILLS AND DRILLS

D1450847

Rich Grawer
Sally Tippett Rains

COACHES
CHOICE™

ISBN: 1-58518-855-7
Library of Congress Control Number: 2003103854
Book layout and diagrams: Deborah Oldenburg
Developmental editor: Hans Schmidt
Text photos: Drew McDaniel and Bob Brooks
Cover design: Kerry Hartjen
Front cover photo: Northwest Sports Photography

Coaches Choice
PO Box 1828
Monterey, CA 93942
www.coacheschoice.com

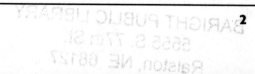

DEDICATION

For my dad, Tony, who through great personal sacrifice, gave me the opportunities in my grade school and high school years to develop my love and appreciation for sports and the values they impart.

– Rich Grawer

ACKNOWLEDGMENTS

Thanks to the following people without whose efforts
this book would not have been possible:

Brian Grawer, Manoli Potsou, and Michael Musick for helping demonstrate the
fundamentals of the game in the book's photos.

Drew McDaniel, a Clayton High School Student, for his professional skill in
photographing the action shots in the book.

All the fine players I have had the privilege of coaching at the
high school and collegiate levels.

All the young men and women who have attended my basketball camps
and clinics over the last 30 years, providing me with wonderful teaching
opportunities and examples of the effectiveness of my teaching methods.

My many assistant coaches, without whose help I never would
have been able to enjoy and succeed in my profession.

My wife, Theresa, for her role in keeping the family together when
I was out pursuing my love of coaching.

My six children—Rick, Shelly, Kevin, Laura, Tim, and Brian—for being
the pride and joy of my life and the best student-athletes
I have ever been associated with.

—Rich Grawer

CONTENTS

The purpose of this book is to help kids, parents, and coaches learn the game of basketball. Too often, players go out to practice on their own and do not know what to do or how to do it. They simply go out in their backyard and shoot the basketball, and then shoot it incorrectly without actually accomplishing much. Parents often want to help their kids to become better basketball players, but they do not know what to teach, how to teach it, or how to make sure that the youngster is practicing a skill the correct way. Many coaches simply take the job because no one else will do it. They have to rush to the library and try to find several books to help them teach the basic skills of the game.

This book will help in all of these situations. No matter if the youngster is 8 or 18, this book contains drills, activities, and pictures that explain all the skills necessary to take a kid and help him become an actual basketball player. Even a youngster can pick up this book and see how to practice the *correct* skills of the game.

Coaches can use this book not only to teach skills, but also to learn how to set up and run a practice session—with or without a gym—to address parents' concerns, and to make the game fun for kids. No matter if you are a coach of a youth league team, junior high, or high school team, you will find what you need in *Youth Basketball Drills and Skills*.

CHAPTER 1

Basketball Stance and Footwork

The legendary Pete Newell has stated that, "During the course of a game a basketball player will handle the ball 10 percent of the time, but he will use his feet 100 percent of the time." With this in mind, it is incumbent upon the coach at any level to utilize drills that help develop *stance* and *footwork*. The coach must remember that every offensive and defensive drill that he implements is a stance or footwork drill. This chapter will focus on stance and three aspects of offensive footwork: the jump stop, the pivot, and the cut, otherwise known as the change of pace, change of direction.

Teaching Stance

Players do very little in basketball without first getting into a *basketball stance*. It is important for them to learn this position because it is the position from which they dribble, jump, pass, catch, slide to defend, and prepare to shoot. The players begin with their feet shoulder-width apart, their backs relatively straight, and their knees flexed. Their knees and shoulders should be pointed straight ahead, not to one side or the other. The players' hands should be held in front of their chest with their palms facing forward and their fingers pointed up, keeping their elbows close to their body. Their heads should be slightly forward and centered over their feet so that a string dropped from their noses would land in the middle of an imaginary line between their feet (Figures 1-1a and 1-1b).

Figure 1-1a

Figure 1-1b

This position is not a natural one. At first it will be difficult for the players and place a lot of stress on the muscles of their thighs. Players need to train their muscles to accept and memorize this stance so they can get into this position quickly on the court whenever it is necessary. During games they will not have time to think about getting into the proper position; the stance should become second nature to them.

One of the best drills to teach players how to get into a stance is to have them sit in an imaginary chair while leaning against a wall. They should have their backs pressed flat against the wall and their butts down with their legs bent at a 90-degree angle and their thighs parallel to the floor. Their feet are shoulder-width apart and their head is centered over their belly button. Their hands are up and active trying to deflect an imaginary pass (Figure 1-2a and 1-2b). Have the players start out by sitting in this stance for 10 seconds, then slowly build up until they can execute it for at least 40 seconds to a minute. The next step in this process is to have the players stay in this stance without leaning against the wall.

Figure 1-2a

Figure 1-2b

The Stance Game or Cutthroat

The *stance game*, or *cutthroat*, is used to reinforce the fundamentals of the stance. The objective is to score points by preventing the offense from scoring. Consequently, a team will want to play defense as long as possible. However, if during the course of the game a defensive player gets out of stance, the coach blows the whistle and that defensive team is off and offense becomes defense. If the defensive team should give up a score, then the offense moves to defense and a new offensive team enters play.

Cutthroat can also be played with an emphasis on offense, i.e., if a player does not triple threat that is tantamount to not being in stance. Thus, the offensive team has forfeited the chance to play offense and they must leave the court and a new team enters play.

Teaching Footwork

To execute a *jump stop*, a player goes from a running motion to a short hop and lands with both feet hitting the ground at the same time (Figures 1-3a and 1-3b).

When a player executes a jump stop his feet should be shoulder-width apart, knees flexed, butt low, head over his belly button, with his hands up. A well-executed jump stop enables a player to be on balance and establish either foot for a pivot.

Figure 1-3a

Figure 1-3b

The *front pivot* and the *reverse pivot* are the two kinds of pivots. To execute the front pivot, a player pivots in a forward motion on the ball of his foot (Figure 1-4). The offensive player should keep the ball close to his body and pivot in a strong aggressive manner. Executing a reverse pivot requires that the player throw his elbow opposite his pivot foot behind him, i.e., on the reverse pivot the player leads with his elbow. On both the front and reverse pivot the player wants to keep his seat down, elbows out, feet shoulder-width apart, protect the ball, and pivot into a strong balanced position.

Figure 1-4

A player will make a number of different *cuts* during the course of a game. Nonetheless, a player must stay low, be on balance, and push off the foot opposite the direction he is going, i.e., if he wants to get open on the left side of the court, he must run to his right and push off his right foot and explode to the left side (Figures 1-5a and 1-5b). Plus, with each cut a player makes, he must vary his speed. This will keep the defense off balance.

Figure 1-5a

Figure 1-5b

In the following pages you will find drills that isolate and illustrate the jump stop, the pivot, and the cut. However, as previously stated, every drill is a stance or footwork drill.

The Jump Stop Drill

Objective: To provide balance in shooting, stopping, screening, passing, and pivoting. All good players are exceptional at the jump stop.

Description: Place four lines on the baseline about five-feet apart. On the coach's whistle, the players in the front of the line will sprint and execute a jump stop at the free-throw line and free-throw line extended. The coach needs to make sure players are on balance, i.e., none are leaning forward or rocking back on their heels; their eyes need to be forward with their head centered over their belly button (Figures 1-6). On the coach's next whistle, the players at the free-throw line will sprint to the half-court line and execute another jump stop (Figure 1-7). The players who are second in line will sprint to the free-throw line and execute a jump stop. Players move on each whistle and execute jump stops at opposite free-throw line and opposite baseline. This drill should be done three to five times a week for two to four minutes a day.

Coaching Points: The coach needs to make sure the players stay low and take an explosive step forward when they come out of their jump stops. They should not stand!

Figure 1-6

Figure 1-7

The Pivot Drill

Description: This drill is set up and run just like the jump stop drill. However, when the players get to the free-throw line, they are to execute either a front pivot or reverse pivot on each whistle (Figure 1-8). A coach must make sure that the players stay low and pivot aggressively. Having players dribble a basketball, jump stop, pivot, and then execute a ball fake before going to the next line can enhance this drill.

Coaching Points: The coach needs to make sure that players *explode forward* or make a positive step after they pivot. He also needs to make sure that the players are not shuffling their feet as they come out of their pivot. If a player is shuffling his feet or changing his pivot foot during the drill, the coach can place a hand on the player's pivot foot to remind him to step with the other foot. This drill should be done in conjunction with the jump stop drill two to four minutes a day about three to five times a week. Great players have great footwork!

Figure 1-8

The Cut Drill

Description: This drill is set up and run just like the jump stop drill. The players start out on the baseline and run to their right. After they have taken three to four steps to their right, they then push off their outside foot and change direction. They will go three or four steps in this new direction and then push off their outside foot and cut in a new direction.

Coaching Points: The coach needs to make sure that players *explode forward* or make a positive step out of their cut. He also needs to make sure that the players have their hands up and are calling for the ball. Lastly, the players need to think of this drill in terms of *change of pace, change of direction*. That is, the players need to vary their speeds going in and out of their cuts.

CHAPTER 2

Dribbling

The *dribble* is a great weapon that unfortunately has always been abused, misused, and overused. Many players have a tendency to fancy themselves as dribblers when in reality they are only bouncers of the ball.

This chapter will discuss the fundamentals of dribbling as well as some guidelines for dribbling. The difference between the two is that *fundamentals* are how a player executes the skill, while *guidelines* are how to become skilled or efficient at executing the skill.

When dribbling a player must have his head and eyes looking forward, his knees must be flexed, and the he must control the ball by the pads on his fingers. Typically the ball should not come any higher than his waist. However, a speed dribble may warrant the ball coming higher. A player must be able to dribble the ball at a speed that enables him to move, stop, and change direction and pace without losing control. A very good ball handler will be able to do all these things at a high speed. The following are guidelines for dribbling the ball:

- A player should dribble to advance the ball up court, penetrate, improve a passing angle, escape trouble, or for screen-and-roll.

- A dribbler should not drive to the baseline unless he has a clear lane to the basket.

- A dribbler needs to keep his head erect and see everyone.

- When dribbling against pressure in a half-court situation, use the non-dribbling arm to form a shield against defensive pressure.
- A player should pick up his dribble with his balance hand.
- A dribbler should stay out of congested areas and away from sidelines and corners.
- A player should never pick up his dribble on either side of the half-court line.
- A player shouldn't dribble with his back to the basket.
- A player should dribble below his waist for protection and control, and should dribble high to his chest for speed—but either way he should always be in control.
- On a low dribble, the player's elbow should be kept almost in contact with his body with his forearm parallel to the floor.
- A player should make his dribble take him somewhere.
- A dribbler's head-and-shoulder fakes are better than ball fakes to set the defensive man up.

The following pages outline a number of *dribbling drills*. These drills will teach and aid in the mastering of handling the basketball. Some of these drills are done with a mass group, some are done 1-on-1 throughout the court, and some are done in small groups.

Teaching Ball Handling

To teach proper ball handling to players, it is important that a coach keep in mind that dribbling is a difficult skill requiring the body to move in rhythm with a moving object. Thus, the coach may want to start with some stationary single- ball drills to help the players develop confidence and a feel for the basketball.

Depending on the level, the coach may start out his players simply dribbling in place. The coach should make sure the ball handlers have their knees bent, head up, and that their dribble hand is on top of the ball. In the beginning players may have a tendency to look at the ball as they dribble. This will result in poor technique, and the coach should be ready to correct this flaw before it becomes a habit. Once the players have demonstrated proficiency dribbling with their strong hand, the coach should have them dribble in place with their weak hand.

The next step with the nascent ball handler is to have him walk the court dribbling with his right hand, then come back dribbling with his left. The coach needs to make sure that the ball never comes higher than the waist and that the dribblers eyes are up seeing the entire court. Once the players have practiced walking and dribbling, it is time for them to pick up the pace. At this point a number of problems can occur. For instance, players can lose control of the ball very quickly because they are moving too fast. A coach needs to remind players to slow down and to keep the ball low. A good motto to use when reminding players to stay low is: *The lower the hips are, the lower the ball goes.* However, the coach still needs to remind players to push themselves to improve their game.

Types of Dribbles

For a player to be complete, he must master a number of dribbles. These dribbles include: the *low-protective dribble*, the *high-speed dribble*, the *power dribble*, the *onside dribble*, the *stutter or hesitation dribble*, the *crossover*, the *wrap around or around the back*, the *spin move*, and lastly, *through the legs*.

The Low-Protective Dribble

In the low-protective dribble, the dribbler is balanced at the knees and the waist (Figure 2-1). When players are excellent dribblers, it is hard to see their hands separate from the ball. Players should protect the ball with their body in the basic basketball position, keeping their body between the ball and the defender.

Figure 2-1

Players should pump the ball downward and, as they make contact, flick their wrist. They have to make sure they hit the ball hard enough to come back up when it hits the floor. Their hand should stay with the ball. Good dribblers put their hands on the side of the ball. This technique is difficult for beginners, but as players improve, they can use the side of the ball to guide it better, to fake better, and to better keep the defense honest and away from them. The following are two drills to help teach the low-protective dribble.

The Protecting-in-a-Rectangle Drill

Description: The coach should mark a rectangle on the floor with tape, approximately two feet by one-and-a-half feet. One player dribbles the ball and another tries to steal it. The dribbler must stay in the rectangle. This drill teaches players to protect the ball in a small, confined area by keeping their body between the ball and the defender (Figure 2-2).

Figure 2-2

The Dribble-Tag Drill

Description: The coach should divide the team into pairs. The first pair is given basketballs and instructed to dribble in the three-second lane while trying to knock the other player's basketball away. This drill forces the players to stay down in a low, protective dribble stance, while keeping their head up to see where the other player is. As players get better with the low-protective dribble, coaches can place three, four, or even five players in the lane dribbling basketballs and trying to knock the ball away from their teammates. Once a ball is knocked out of the lane, that player is eliminated. The one player left dribbling is the winner (Figure 2-3).

The High-Speed Dribble

The second dribble is the high-speed dribble (Figure 2-4). This dribble is different from the low-protective dribble because the dribbler is trying to explode past the defense and either drive to the basket or get an open shot. This dribble is often used in fast-break situations by point guards who have to get the ball up the floor quickly. The dribble must be higher and harder than the low-protective dribble simply because the player is moving quickly past the defense, trying to escape the defender.

Players should dribble the ball waist high or slightly higher, and put it out in front of themselves and to the side so they won't kick it as they increase their speed. They should also have their heads up to find the open man. Coaches need to have players practice this dribble with both their right and left hand. The following are two drills to help teach the high-speed dribble.

Figure 2-3

Figure 2-4

The Sideline High-Speed Drill

Description: Each player is given a basketball and lined up along the sideline or a taped line on the court with both feet on the left side of the line. The players dribble the basketball on the right side of the line, first walking, then jogging, then going full speed. This drill enables the coach to look right down the line and see which players are not putting the ball out in front and to the side. If the ball is not dribbled out in front and to the side on the high-speed dribble, the player will probably either outrun the ball or kick it. Next, the players start with both feet on the right side of the sideline and dribble the ball on the left side of the line with their left hand. Players should dribble while standing, then walking, then jogging, then sprinting. Again, coaches should emphasize that the ball should be slightly out in front and to the side of the player (Figure 2-5).

Variation: Another drill that can be used to teach the high-speed dribble is the full-court dribbling drill, in which the player dribbles down the court with the right hand and returns using the left.

Coaching Point: An excellent combination drill to teach both the low-protective and high-speed dribble is the circle drill.

Figure 2-5

The Circle Drill

Description: Players line up under the basket, each with a ball. They should use the high-speed dribble everywhere except when going around the circle. When dribbling around the three circles, the player should slow down and glide around the circle using the low-protective dribble. When the players reach the other end of the court and come around that circle for the last time, they explode to the basket with a high-speed dribble and shoot a lay-up (Figure 2-6).

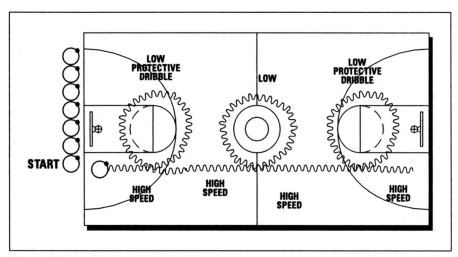

Figure 2-6

The Power Dribble

Because of their position near the basket, and because they are usually the tallest or strongest players on the court, defenses tend to sag around post players, dropping two or even three defenders to the post. For this reason, post players need to learn a type of dribble different from those used by other players on the team. The high-speed dribble is not appropriate in the post area. Coaches should teach post players one simple dribble: the power dribble.

After post players receive the ball and chest it properly, they should try to make a play using the power dribble (Figure 2-7). To execute the power dribble, post players take a drop step and pound the ball hard off the floor so when they catch the ball, it will be close to their body at about waist level. When the power dribble is performed properly, with the ball thrown hard against the floor, it will come back up so fast that it almost appears as if it never left the player's hands. If post players can learn to coordinate their foot movement with this dribble, they present a formidable offensive threat. The power dribble gives them momentum as they go to the basket. Coaches should also teach post players to never try to dribble the ball away from their body or above their waist unless they have an unimpeded path to the basket.

The Onside Dribble

The first dribble move that should follow the low-protective and high-speed dribble is the onside dribble (Figures 2-8a and 2-8b). The ball is dribbled with the right hand while the dribbler is facing the defender. The dribbler then fakes everything—head, shoulder, and foot—to the left, but keeps the ball to the right. As the defender reacts to the fake left, the dribbler explodes by on the right side toward the basket.

The best way to teach the onside dribble is to mark off a rectangle with tape for each player. The player stands in the rectangle and begins to dribble the ball outside the rectangle with his right hand. Upon the coach's command of *fake*, the player fakes left with his head, shoulder, and foot while keeping the ball to the right.

The next step in the teaching process is to have players walk while dribbling the basketball. The coach places a chair 25 to 30 feet out on the court. When the players reach the chair, they execute the onside fake to the left and explode by the chair on the right.

Coaches can vary the drill by placing several chairs on the court for players to fake at, or by having players dribble with their left hand so they fake right and explode by on the left.

Figure 2-7

Figure 2-8a

Figure 2-8b

Final Pointers on the Onside Dribble

As dribblers execute the fakes in one direction, they have a tendency to get off balance. Raising the dribble slightly will enable players to maintain their balance.

If players become proficient with the onside dribble, they can next learn to bring the basketball slightly to the left, while faking left, by placing their right hand on the left side of the ball as if going left. They then quickly switch the hand to the right side of the ball, moving it back to the right. This technique is especially effective because many defenders watch the basketball. Moving the ball first to the left and then quickly back to the right improves the player's chance of escaping the defender. This maneuver is extremely difficult, and should be practiced only after mastering the basic techniques.

The Stutter Dribble

The stutter dribble is used in a fast-break situation. It is a change-of-pace dribble that is the result of a ball handler dribbling quickly, then slowing down as he approaches the defender by stuttering or squeaking his shoes, and then exploding by the defender body-to-body. (The term *body-to-body* means that the offensive player wants to go by the defender as close as possible to eliminate any chance of defensive recovery).

The basic fundamentals of the stutter dribble are that the ball handler must be moving at a high rate of speed and on balance as he approaches the defender. The basketball must be no higher than his hips and in general, the lower the dribble, the better it is. His feet are stuttered by taking three to six short choppy steps. The coach will know the players are executing the stutter correctly if he hears the players' shoes squeak on the wooden floor when they stutter step. The last fundamental of the stutter step is that the offensive player must explode out of his stutter steps and go by the defender body-to-body. The offensive player must watch the defender to see if he reaches for the ball or begins to stand—if any of these two defensive lapses occur, then it is the precise time for the offensive player to shift gears and go by the defender body-to-body.

The Crossover Dribble

The crossover dribble is a change-of-direction, change-of-pace dribble. This dribble can be used in full and half-court situations, and if it is mastered can be a devastating weapon. The basic fundamental for the crossover requires that a player change hands by urgently pushing the ball from one side of his body to the other. When the ball is pushed it must be pushed close to his body and towards his back foot. This will keep the ball away from the defender. When the ball passes in front of the dribbler's body it must be kept low. A good rule of thumb is to not let the ball come any higher than the dribbler's kneecaps. The key to making the crossover an effective is weapon is that the ball handler must not only change hands on the crossover, but also change direction. This will keep the defense off balance.

The Wrap Around or Around the Back

The wrap around is most effective when combined with a stutter dribble. Nonetheless, when used properly it can be a great escape dribble in a full-court situation. The essential fundamental to the wrap around dribble is that the ball handler must slap his opposite *butt cheek* when executing this dribble. In other words, if the dribbler is going around his back from his right to his left, he must push the ball from his right to his left hand and slap his left cheek with his right hand (Figure 2-9). This will ensure that the ball is not pushed too far away from his body on the wrap around. As always, the ball handler must be low, head up, and on balance. Keep in mind that the novice ball handler will want to move his head and body to try to find the ball. Encourage the players to resist this temptation and to instead push the ball around their waist and to the front of the body without looking.

Figure 2-9

The Spin Move

The spin move is executed in transition. The fundamentals of the spin move require that the ball handler change direction by stepping into the defender with the leg opposite the dribbling hand, and then doing a reverse pivot while changing dribbling hands. The ball must be kept close to his body and his head must snap forward into the new direction. This will enable the ball handler to see any on coming defenders, as well as any open teammates.

Through the Legs

The through-the-legs dribble requires many of the fundamentals of the other dribble moves, but instead of pushing the ball in front of the body, as in the crossover, or behind the body, as in the wrap around, this dribble requires that the ball be pushed between the legs. When the dribble is executed the ball handler must stay low, push the ball between his legs, and then continue to accelerate in a new direction (Figures 2-10a and 2-10b). If the ball handler rises while doing the through the legs dribble, he might get the ball stolen.

Figure 2-10a

Figure 2-10b

Drills to Teach Dribble Moves

The Dribbling-at-a-Cone Drill

Objective: To practice the proper footwork and timing of the dribble moves, as well as transitioning from moving quickly to slowing down, and then back to moving quickly.

Equipment Needed: Each player will need a ball and the coach will need three cones.

Description: A cone is placed at the free-throw line, the half-court line, and at the opposite free-throw line. The players are in line on the baseline. The drill begins by having the first player in line use a high-speed dribble at the first cone. As he approaches the cone, he then executes the desired dribble move. After the move is executed, he then continues to accelerate and goes back to the high-speed dribble. He will continue with his high-speed dribble until he approaches another cone at which time he will repeat the move. Once all the players have gone in one direction with their right hand, they should go the other direction with their left hand.

Coaching Points: The coach needs to make sure the players have their heads up and are not looking at the ball. He also needs to pay attention to the fact that when players are first learning a dribble move, the tendency is for the player to sacrifice correct execution for speed. Thus, the coach needs to remind players that speed will come after the player has learned to properly execute the move.

The Dribbling-Between-Chairs Drill

Objective: To practice the proper footwork and timing of the move, as well as transitioning from moving quickly to slowing down, and then back to moving quickly. Also, because the ball handler has to go between two narrowly separated chairs, he begins to practice cutting closely by a defender.

Equipment Needed: Each player will need a ball and the coach will need two folding chairs.

Description: The two chairs are placed at the top of the key about three- to five-feet apart. The players will be in line at half-court. On the coach's command, the first player will begin speed dribbling at one of the chairs. As he approaches the chair he is to go to his dribble move and then explode out of the move and go between the chairs (Figures 2-11a and 2-11b). The coach is to remind the players to cut as close as possible to the chair. By using two chairs the coach can increase or decrease the space that the ball handler is going through and thereby help the player develop the concept of going by the defender body-to-body. If a player knocks over a chair, then the player knows that he is developing a stutter move that will prohibit the defender from recovering.

Figure 2-11a

Figure 2-11b

Coaching Points: As in any ball-handling drill, the coach needs to make sure the players are under control and on balance. However, the coach needs to be aware that a fine line exists between the player who is going slowly to learn how to do the skill, and the player who is going slowly because he is lazy. In any practice session a coach should have a segment where he tells the players to go as fast as they can and not worry about mistakes. This will encourage the players to go game speed and gain confidence in the move.

Basic Drills to Develop Ball Handling

The best way to improve dribbling skills is to practice dribbling with two basketballs. This section will discuss six two-ball dribbling drills.

The Dribbling Two Balls While Standing in One Place Drill

Description: Each player has two basketballs (if you have a shortage of balls then have the players pair up). Begin the drill by having the players dribble the two balls simultaneously. The coach must make sure that the ball handler's eyes are up, that his knees are flexed, and that the balls come no higher than his hips. Also, he should dribble the basketballs on the pads of his fingers (Figure 2-12). Have the players go in 30-second intervals and then switch with their partner.

Coaching Points: Remind the players that the lower their hips go, the lower the ball goes. This drill should be done everyday as part of a ball-handling segment in practice.

The Two-Ball Alternate Dribble Drill

Description: The players should stand in place, but instead of having both balls hit the ground at the time like the previous drill, they will alternate them. All the dribbling fundamentals are the same: eyes up, keep the balls below the hips, knees flexed, butt down, and the balls on the pads of the fingers (Figure 2-13).

Figure 2-12

Figure 2-13

Coaching Points: To demonstrate the importance of keeping the ball below the hips, have the players stand straight up and try this drill. Balls will bounce all over the place. Explain to the kids that the lower their hips are the smaller the margin for error. Conversely, when the players stand, the margin for error increases and causes the loss of control of the balls. This drill should be done for 30 to 60 seconds everyday.

The Two-Ball Simultaneous Speed- Dribble Drill

Description: Have five groups of two players on the baseline. Have players two-ball dribble simultaneously as fast as they can to the free-throw line or the half-court line and back. When they reach the baseline have the ball handlers give the balls to the next person in line. The coach must make sure that the ball handler's eyes are up, that his knees are flexed, and that the balls come no higher than his hips. Also, he should dribble the basketballs on the pads of his fingers.

Coaching Points: The taller players will have a difficult time with this drill. Have these players start out with a walk, build up to a jog, and work up to a full sprint. If some players can already do this drill have them go at angles or have them go backwards. To make this drill useful, the coach must remind the players to see the floor; they should not stare at the ball. This drill should be done for 30 to 60 seconds everyday.

Two-Ball Alternate Speed-Dribble Drill

Description: Have five groups of two players on the baseline. Have players two-ball alternate dribble as fast at they can to the free-throw line or the half-court line and back. When they reach the baseline have the ball handlers give the balls to the next person in line. The coach must make sure that the ball handler's eyes are up, that his knees are flexed, and that the balls come no higher than his hips. Also, he should dribble the basketballs on the pads of his fingers.

Coaching Points: The taller players will have a difficult time with this drill. Have these players start out with a walk, build up to a jog, and work up to a full sprint. If some players can already do this drill have them go at angles or have them go backwards. To make this drill useful, the coach must remind the players to stay low and keep the basketballs below their hips. This drill should be done for 30 to 60 seconds everyday.

Two-Ball Spin-Moves Drill

Description: Have five groups of two players on the baseline. Have players two-ball dribble to the half court line. However, in this drill the players will not dribble in straight lines. Instead, they will dribble at angles. When a player changes directions he is to execute a spin move. The players must keep the balls low on the spin. Have the players exchange basketballs when they return to the baseline.

Coaching Points: The taller players will have a difficult time with this drill. Have these players start out with a walk, build up to a jog, and work up to a full sprint. Make sure that on the spin move the ball handlers snap their head in the direction that they are executing the spin move. This will ensure that the ball handler can see up the floor and not stare at the ball. This drill should be done for 30 to 60 seconds everyday.

Two-Ball Spin-Moves Against-a- Defender Drill

Description: This drill requires two lines on the baseline. The ball handlers will dribble two basketballs for the length of the court, but this time they will be going against a defender. The defender's job is to make the ball handler change direction and thereby use the spin move. When all players have gone the length of the court, have the players switch offense to defense and dribble back to the original baseline.

Coaching Points: Do not allow defensive players to use their hands and have ball handlers match up with players of similar skills, i.e., do not have your post players work against your speedy guards. This drill should be done for 30 to 60 seconds everyday.

Remember that any dribble drill that uses one ball can be converted to a two-ball dribble drill. The coach must remember to tell the players to execute the proper fundamentals when dribbling. He also needs to remind the players that any offensive drill that involves dribbling is a dribbling drill.

Dribble Games

During the course of a season it is incumbent upon the coach to develop drills that will not only work on fundamentals, but that will also provide variety and change for practice. Variety will keep the players interested and energetic and will make for a more productive practice. This section discusses two dribble games that can be done at some point during the season to keep practice interesting.

Game One: Full-Court Dribble Relays

Description: Players are broken up into even teams. The players should then one-ball dribble or two-ball dribble the length of the court. Determine if the players can alternate dribble or simultaneous dribble. The team that has everyone in his line go up and back first wins.

Coaching Points: Have the kids execute different moves in the relay, i.e., spin moves, crossover, around the back, through the legs. All these moves can be executed with two basketballs. Have the winning team get a drink first or get out of a sprint, etc. Make sure players do not cheat by tossing the ball way ahead and then catching up to it.

Game Two: Dribble Knockout

Description: All the players have a ball and are placed in a confined area, i.e., on one-half of the court, inside the three-point line, etc. The purpose of the game is to have the players dribble and try to knock one of their teammates basketballs out of the confined area. As the group of ball handlers becomes smaller and smaller, move them to a smaller area, i.e., the jump circle or the key area.

Coaching Points: Make sure players keep their heads up and work on staying low while playing this game. Have the winning team get a drink first or get out of a sprint, etc. Have the players practice all the previously described dribbling techniques.

CHAPTER 3

Passing, Catching, and Cutting

Passing is probably the least worked on aspect of basketball by coaches and players. Not only are the fundamentals of passing important, but players should be taught when they should pass rather than dribble or shoot. Players should also understand that passing advances the basketball more quickly than the dribble. The guidelines for passing the ball are:

- Players should add ball fakes.
- Players should not jump pass.
- Players should not pass across the lane.
- Receivers must always break hard to the ball.
- Communication is vital—passers call the receiver's name; receivers call the passer's name.
- Players should time their passes so the man in motion doesn't have to stop and wait for the ball.
- Players should not pass off the dribble.

During the course of a game a player will be asked to throw a number of different passes from a variety of angles. As a consequence, each pass has specific fundamentals.

The core fundamentals of passing require that a player must be on balance, knees flexed, butt down, eyes up and strong with the ball. On all passes the passer must pass the ball away from the defense and follow through. He must also pass the ball to a player who can be productive in a specific area of the floor. The specific fundamentals for each type of pass are as follows.

The Two-Handed Chest Pass

Description: The passer must be in a triple-threat position, knees flexed, and butt down. His hands must be on the outside of the ball, as opposed to below, behind, or on top. The passer must step to his receiver and push the ball out away from his chest. By rotating his wrists down, the passer puts backspin on the ball and has the proper follow-through to help ensure that the pass will get to the receiver (Figures 3-1a and 3-1b). This pass is often used to inbound the ball against pressure.

Coaching Points: Make sure the passer steps to the receiver and stays low. If the passer is in a vertical position and does not step to his receiver, he will not be able to pass with much strength and the pass is more likely to be stolen.

Figure 3-1a

Figure 3-1b

The Two-Handed Bounce Pass

Description: Bounce passes are executed in much the same way as the chest pass, but this pass requires that the ball is bounced off the floor rather than travel strictly through the air. The key on the two-handed bounce pass is that the passer is trying to hit a spot on the floor about two-thirds of the way to the receiver. The pass should hit the receiver in the numbers area. The passer should step to the receiver, stay low, and follow through on the pass (Figures 3-2a and 3-2b).

Coaching Points: Have the players throw a pass too close to the receiver and too far away. Have the passer note how difficult it is to catch a bounce pass to close to the receiver. Also, have the passer throw a pass that is too far away from the receiver and note how slowly the ball moves to the receiver.

Figure 3-2a

Figure 3-2b

The One-Handed Push Pass

Description: To execute the push pass, the passer must get his hand behind the ball and push it in the direction he wishes it to go. The ball must roll off his fingertips of the pass hand and the passer must step in the direction of his pass. This pass can be thrown as either an air or bounce pass. The push pass is often used when the passer must step around the defense to pass the ball. Lastly, the passer must be low and stepping to the receiver when making this pass. See Figure 3-3.

Coaching Points: Ball fakes are essential to completing passes. When passing the ball, either low-fake high or high-fake low.

Figure 3-3

Catching

Before teaching youngsters how to pass the basketball, it is important for coaches to determine whether they know how to catch the basketball. When catching the ball, players should open their palms and have them facing the passer. They should spread their fingers evenly, creating a larger surface to receive the ball. The thumbs should be six- to eight-inches apart. The receiver should always step toward the incoming pass, catch it with his arms extended, and then draw the ball inward to his chest. The player then pivots, faces the basket, and gets into triple-threat position. The following drills will help young players become better receivers.

Good Hands Drills

The Pound Drill

Description: Players take a basketball and pound it back and forth between their hands. They should do this as hard as they can to toughen up their hands.

The Two-Man Passing Drill

Objective: To teach effective passing and receiving.

Description: The team is divided into pairs. The partners pass the ball back and forth, concentrating on a specific pass—chest pass, bounce pass, or overhead pass. Passers should bend their knees and step toward the receiver, passing the ball to the outside hand. Receivers should step toward the ball and the passer. Most passes should arrive between the receiver's waist and chest.

The Over-the-Shoulder Toss

Description: Players hold the ball out in front of their right shoulder at shoulder height. They then toss the ball directly over their right shoulder and try to catch it with both hands behind their back (Figure 3-4). As soon as their fingers feel the ball, they should squeeze and hold it. The drill is not effective if the ball is tossed in such a way that players arch their back and let the ball roll down their back.

Figure 3-4

The Blind-Catch Drill

Description: Players stand at the block with their back to the coach, who has assumed a position on the wing. Players should be in a good basketball position with their hands ready in front of their chest. When the coach yells, "Now," the players execute a quick 180-degree jump turn, landing in a balanced position with their feet and shoulders squared to the coach, who makes the pass. The receivers catch the ball, draw it to their chest, and execute a lay-up at the basket.

Coaching Points: The coach can vary the timing of the pass depending upon the athletic ability of the player. Passing the ball while the jump turn is being executed will force the player to really concentrate on the fundamentals of catching. Passing the ball a split second before the player jump turns also improves catching agility, coordination, quickness, and balance. Many younger players are scared of this drill because they do not want the ball to hit them. The coach should take the time to reassure them and remind them that if their hands are properly aligned in front of their chest, palms facing forward with their thumbs about eight-inches apart, the ball will hit their hands. With practice, they will learn to catch it.

The Jump-and-Catch Drill

Equipment Needed: The coach should place obstacles such as cones or small hurdles on the floor.

Description: As players jump over the obstacles, the coach makes a chest pass to them. Players should execute the jump, watch the pass, catch the ball on the floor or while airborne, and return it to the coach with a good chest pass.

The Backboard Blind-Catch Drill

Description: Players stand about 8 to 10 feet in front of the rim with their backs to the basket, facing the coach, who is standing at the free-throw line. The coach yells, "Now," and fires the ball off the backboard as the player executes a quick jump turn. Players should catch the ball off the board and then shoot a lay-up.

Coaching Point: The coach should assess the athletic ability of each player to determine how hard and high the pass off the backboard will be.

Competitive Passing Drills

The Bull-in-the-Ring Drill

Description: Three players are positioned around the circle as shown in Figure 3-5. A defensive player tries to deflect the basketball as it is passed among the three players. The three offensive players are required to stay in triple-threat position; use short, crisp pass fakes; and use bounce, chest, and overhead passes. If the offensive players have to move from their position to catch a pass, then it is considered a bad pass and the player who made the pass must take the defender's place. If the defender deflects a pass, the person who made the pass becomes the defender.

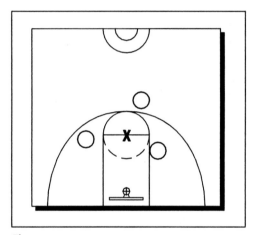

Figure 3-5

The No-Touch Passing Drill

Objective: To combine the ideas of guarding the basket and challenging the ball handler to deflect a pass, forcing the defender to make a quick judgment and then react.

Description: Players are aligned as shown in Figure 3-6, with guards in a line near half-court and defenders positioned outside the baseline. The guards dribble into the top of the circle area. As soon as they enter this area (the shaded area in Figure 3-6), the defender can challenge the ball. The ball handler must stop between the top of the key and the free- throw line and is challenged by the defender in this area. All the defender must do to be successful is touch the ball. Once the defender touches the ball, the next player in each line steps into the drill.

Coaching Points: The defender may fake at the dribbler and fake back to play the other offensive player stationed at the block. That offensive player cannot move from the spot. In this situation, the dribbler can either shoot or attempt a quick pass to the player on the block, and the defender reacts appropriately. The drill encourages quick thinking, quick feet, quick hands, and quick reactions on the part of the defender, as well as good passing judgment and techniques.

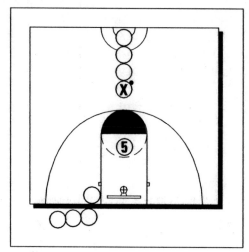

Figure 3-6

The Two-Ball Passing Drill

Objective: To emphasize coordination, agility, timing, and spacing.

Description: Players should line up as shown in Figures 3-7a and 3-7b with partners facing each other and each player holding a basketball. Partners should pass the ball to each other simultaneously. Theoretically, the two balls should pass each other at the same time. The players should concentrate on catching the pass and returning it. The players should present a target chest high on their left side (if right-handed). Both players must pass with the same hand for this drill to work. Passers should aim at and hit the target. The coach will designate the type of pass to be made. Timing and concentration are essential. Players should catch the pass in the left hand, clasp the right hand over the ball, swing the ball to the right side, and return the pass. They should begin the drill slowly and increase their speed as they gain confidence.

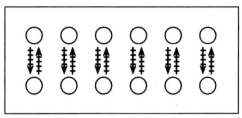

Figure 3-7a

Figure 3-7b

The Two-Man Full-Court Passing Drill

Objective: To emphasize coordination, agility, timing, and spacing.

Description: Players form two lines behind one baseline on either side of the free-throw lane (see Figure 3-8). Each pair of players has a basketball. They run a two-man fast break to the other end, focusing on spacing and timing, and shoot a lay-up off a bounce pass. After each player has shot a lay-up, the players repeat the drill, shooting a jump shot from the elbow of the lane, and finally run the drill shooting a bank jump shot from 8 to 10 feet.

The player with the ball should stop near or inside the three-point line to spread the defense and create good spacing for the bounce pass.

Coaching Point: The coach may choose to add a defender and run a 2-on-1 fast break.

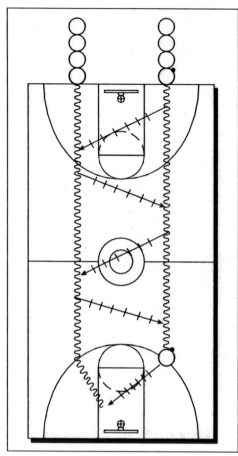

Figure 3-8

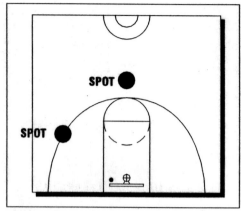

Figure 3-9

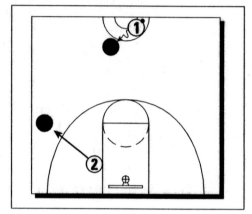

Figure 3-10

Considerations for Creating Better Passers

- Do the players know how to catch a ball? Their palms should be open and facing the passer, and their fingers spread to create a wide target for the ball. They should step to the ball, catch it with their arms extended, and then draw it back toward their chest.

- Timing and spacing are essential to good passing. The pass should be made when the receiver is open and ready to catch it.

- Coaches should teach and develop these concepts of good timing and spacing. For example, the coach can mark spots on the floor as illustrated in Figure 3-9 and run timing drills. When player #1 reaches a designated spot, player #2 pops out to the second spot for a pass (Figure 3-10). The coach can then add a third player (Figure 3-11). Player #1 reaches the designated spot and passes to player #2. Player #4 then goes to his spot to receive a pass.

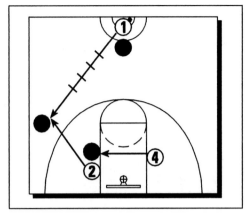

Figure 3-11

Variations to the Timing Drills

The Point-Wing Timing Drill

Description: The point player passes to the wing, fakes to the weakside, and then makes a V-cut down the side of the lane for a return pass (usually a bounce pass) and the lay-up (Figure 3-12).

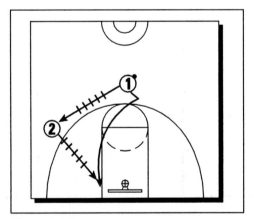

Figure 3-12

The Wing-Post Timing Drill

Description: The wing player passes to the post, then cuts to the baseline or the middle for a short return bounce pass (Figure 3-13).

Coaching Point: The coach may choose to have the wing pass to the post, slide to the baseline for a return pass, and then either take the shot or pass back into the post.

Variations: Two timing drill options for four players are illustrated in Figures 3-14 through 3-16. The point player passes to the strongside wing (Figure 3-14) and cuts to the baseline. The weakside wing moves to the top of the key. The strongside wing has two options. He may pass to player #3, who then passes to the post player cutting across the lane (Figure 3-15). The strongside wing may also make a return pass to the point player who has cut to the baseline, then fake to the elbow of the lane and make a V-cut around the post player to the block (Figure 3-16).

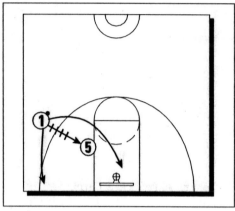

Figure 3-13

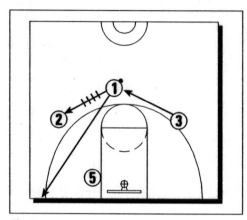

Figure 3-14

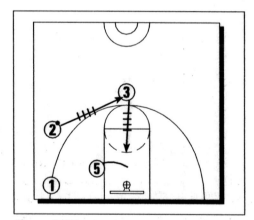

Figure 3-15

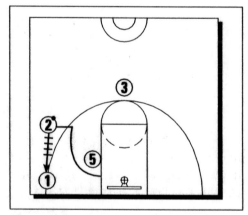

Figure 3-16

Passing Drills without Dribbling

To emphasize the importance of passing in the game of basketball, coaches can set up games in practice in which the players are not allowed to dribble the ball. For example, the coach may have players compete 2-on-2 and require them to move the ball using passes, fakes, and cuts rather than the dribble.

For younger players, coaches can require the offense to make a designated number of consecutive completed passes to gain points. For example, if the offense completes three passes without the defense touching the ball, they earn a point. The coach may also award points for completing passes to specific areas, such as the post area. The coach may also have players work 3-on-3 without dribbling and teach them to screen away from the ball to get players open. Once the players have grasped the importance of passing the ball, the coach can allow them to attempt to score a basket without dribbling. This type of drill forces players to pass, move, cut, and protect the ball, and can be played 2-on-2, 3-on-3, 4-on-4, or 5-on-5. The coach should insist on proper spacing to keep players from congregating in one small area of the court, especially when performing the drill with larger numbers. In trying to create proper spacing, cutting, and movement along with good passing concept, place 5 X's with tape as shown in Figure 3-17.

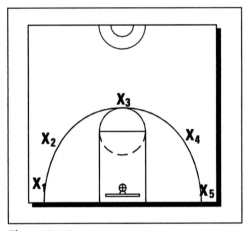

Figure 3-17

Three players are put on the court, on X3, X4, and X2. Start the player at X3 with the basketball. When X3 passes the ball to either X4 or X2, he cuts to another open X on the court—an X that is unoccupied by another player. When a player receives a pass (on an X), he faces the basket and gets into triple-threat position, holding the ball for at least two seconds. The other players are moving to another X on the court. This movement continues for a couple of minutes until the coach stops the action. The rules for movement are simple:

- No two players can occupy the same X at the same time.
- All cutters should always look at the person with the ball so that a possible return pass can be made to that particular cutter.
- When passing players can never skip over an X for example, X2 can pass to X1 or X3, but not to X5. X5 can only pass to X4; X3 could pass to spot X2 or X4.

This drill creates excellent movement and cutting with proper spacing between players. Too often kids do not understand the concept of proper spacing—staying 12 to 15 feet away from teammates. This drill also emphasizes conditioning and triple-threat position, along with passing and catching. The coach should make all players pass the ball to the outside hand of their teammates. The coach can also teach screening away from the ball. Later, coaches can allow the players to use the dribble to get from one spot to another, or to use the dribble to balance out the floor or to help create timing. When satisfied that their players have mastered all of these techniques, coaches can allow the players to shoot the ball off the movement. In reality, what the coach has done is to create the basis for a half-court offense.

Cutting

The ability to cut will help any player and team develop into a strong offensive force. Cutting, like defense, does not necessarily require tons of talent. A player merely needs to be relentless, smart, and patient. The fundamentals of cutting are:

- Players must have their hands up prepared to catch a pass.
- Players must change directions and speeds when cutting.
- The cut is executed by running in one direction, stopping suddenly, then changing direction by planting on the outside foot and turning in the desired direction.
- Players must remember to stay low and call, "ball," when cutting.

The Cut and Square-up Drill

Description: The coach needs to form a line of passers and cutters. If the team is a group of novices, the coach may want to take on the role as full-time passer. Passers each have a ball and are placed at the top of the key. The cutters are in a line at the free-throw line extended. On the coach's command, the first cutter will run hard towards the baseline, stop, plant his outside foot, and cut hard towards the ball. The passer will pass the cutter the ball who will catch the ball, pivot, and face the basket in a triple-threat position. The coach may let the player who cut drive in and shoot a lay-up, or he may have the player simply pass the ball to the next person in line.

Coaching Points: The coach needs to make sure the cutter does not stand when he comes out of his cut and has his hands up and calls, "ball." The cut should also be made at game speed.

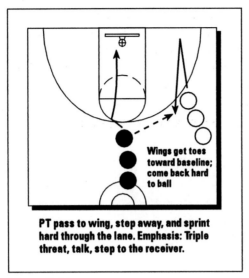

Wings get toes toward baseline; come back hard to ball

PT pass to wing, step away, and sprint hard through the lane. Emphasis: Triple threat, talk, step to the receiver.

Figure 3-18

Faking

Besides passing, catching, and cutting, coaches should also teach their players how to *fake*. The fundamentals for faking are:

- If players are being closely guarded and wish to pass the ball low (the bounce pass), they should fake high.
- If players are being closely guarded and wish to pass the ball high, they should fake the bounce pass low.
- If players wish to pass left, they should fake and look right.
- If players wish to pass right, they should fake and look left.

CHAPTER 4

Rebounding

The quickest way for any team to improve its success is to improve its ability to *rebound*. This fact has been proven in a couple of mantras by basketball's greatest coaches. John Wooden has characterized basketball as a game of possessions. That is, the team that gets the most shots will usually win. Thus, if a team controls the boards, they do get more shots than their opponents and increase their chances of winning. During the Lakers championship run in the 1980s, coach Pat Riley instilled in his weak rebounding players the following maxim: *No rebounds, no rings*. The Lakers realized the importance of rebounding and went on to win five championships in the 1980s.

A player must execute a number of fundamentals when rebounding. First, the defensive player must be between his man and the basket. On the offensive shot, the defender must aggressively pivot into his opponent, keep his butt low, hands up, and be ready to elevate and the grab the ball. The rebounder must explode up toward the ball with both hands, i.e., he should not let the ball come to him; he should go up and snatch it. Also, once the defender has secured the rebound, he must chin the ball and be ready to look upcourt and start the fast break. However, the rebounder must also be aware of any immediate defensive pressure applied by the opponent. Some guidelines that a rebounder has to remember are:

- Assume every shot is going to be missed.
- Do not get pushed too far underneath the basket.

- Be aggressive.
- Seventy percent of all shots rebound opposite the side they are shot.
- Keep the hands up.
- Rebounding takes very little talent.

Many of basketball's greatest rebounders were not necessarily *leapers*. They were very aggressive, determined, and competitive players. The following drills will give the coach a handful of ways of teaching the skill of rebounding in an individual and team setting. However, what the coach must remember is that every drill is a rebounding drill.

Individual Rebounding Drill

Objective: To work on the basic fundamentals of rebounding.

Description: Break the players up into even groups and place them at various baskets around the gym. Each player should have a ball. Have the line form at the free-throw line. The first person in line will throw the ball off the backboard and jump up and grab the rebound. They will then turn and throw a strong outlet pass to a teammate who is standing at the free-throw line extended. Rotate the player by having the rebounder go to the outlet position and the outlet player going to the rebounder line.

Coaching Points: The coach needs to make sure the players are going up aggressively and with two hands. The rebounder should also land on balance and chin the ball. Have the outlet person call out—*outlet!* This will promote communication.

The 1-on-1 In-the-Paint Drill

Description: Have two players in the paint. The offensive player with the ball throws the ball off the glass and goes up to rebound it. When he lands he is to go up strong and shoot it against the defensive player. The offensive player is to concentrate on keeping his hands high, going up aggressively, taking contact on the shot, and finishing the play. Have each player go three times and then switch.

Coaching Points: In this drill, the coach has to instill in his players the importance of the three-point play. The players must go up strong to get the ball and then shoot it. The coach needs to ensure that the players are not fading away from the basket. The coach may also want to do a series where the offensive player, after he lands, executes a shot fake before he goes back up with the ball. The coach should encourage the defender to leave his feet and make contact with the offensive player to help the offense get used to contact.

The Tip Drill

Description: Break the players up into even groups and place them at various baskets. Each player should have a ball. Have the players take turns throwing the ball off the backboard and tipping the ball into the basket. Encourage the players to keep their fingers spread when tipping the ball into the basket. The coach can have the players for a set number of baskets or for a certain time period.

Coaching Points: The coach can make this drill tougher by having the players continually tip the ball off the backboard for a given amount of time. This will teach the players coordination, timing, and conditioning. In fact, the coach may want to do this drill before having the players tip the ball in the basket.

The Blood Alley Drill

(*Note*: This drill should only be done with advanced high school players in the safest of conditions.)

Objective: To teach aggressiveness, improve conditioning, and to see who has heart.

Description: Split the team in half and put the two teams on two different baskets. Put three players in the lane area and the others on the baseline under the basket. The coach will be at the free-throw line with a ball. When the coach shoots the ball, the three players in the lane area fight for the ball and attempt to score off the offensive boards. The other two players must keep the offensive player from scoring. The players will continue to fight in the lane to score and prevent the other man from scoring until a player has scored three points. Once three points have been scored, that player steps off and another player steps into the game. The only rule is that if the ball lands outside the lane area, the ball is then thrown back to the coach who shoots again and the game continues.

Coaching Points: The key to making this drill effective is by having players continuously rotate in. Blood alley is a very difficult drill, and sometimes players will get bloody noses, bloody lips, etc. The coach should not do this drill every day. However, when it is properly timed in practice, it can prove to be an awesome drill.

CHAPTER 5

Lay-ups

Shooting requires that a player make a number of different shots during the course of a game. A player who makes a variety of shots from a variety of places greatly increases his chances of playing. In the next few chapters the focus will be on the fundamentals of three shots: the lay-up, the free throw, and the jump shot. The drills included will fall into three categories: shooting with no pressure, shooting against a time element, and shooting against a defender.

The *lay-up* at first glance may appear to be an easy shot. However, it can be very difficult to execute at times. Elements that increase the difficulty of the lay-up can be such things as defensive pressure, lack of balance, poor angles, concern about drawing a foul, and the possibility of having the shot blocked. But if a player practices lay-ups correctly, from a number of angles and speeds, he will soon develop the confidence he needs to make any kind of lay-up in any kind of situation. The two types of lay-ups are: the *jump-stop lay-up* or power, and the *driving lay-up*.

The jump stop lay-up is the easiest lay-up to learn and maybe the more consistent of the two types of lay-ups. This lay-up is shot in the lane and usually under a lot of defensive pressure. It can also make an off-balance defender commit a foul. It can be even more effective if the offensive player can get his head centered with the rim because then the rim will protect him from defenders on the weakside. The fundamentals of the jump-stop lay-up are:

- The player's shoulders should be square to the backboard.
- The ball is chinned.
- The offensive player explodes straight up, has both hands on the ball, and is prepared for contact from the defense.
- The ball gently comes off the fingertips and softly goes off the backboard and into the hoop.

A running lay-up or driving lay-up is usually shot in a fast-break situation. However, an athletic player with quickness will find that he will often utilize the driving lay-up in the half-court set. The fundamentals of the driving lay-up are:

- The player should take off on the foot opposite the shooting hand, i.e., a left-handed lay-up requires the player to jump off his right foot and vice versa for the right-handed shot.
- The shooter has to jump for height rather than distance on the breakaway lay-up.
- The ball needs to be protected with the non-shooting arm while in the air.
- The palm of the shooting hand ideally will face the backboard at the conclusion of the shot.

However, as players become more skilled they will soon find that they can shoot lay-ups from a variety of angles without consideration of hand placement. Another important element to remember when shooting the lay-up is that the player must take the proper angle to the basket. The proper angle is one in which the player shooting the ball drives between the block and the first hash mark on the lane line. When teaching the lay-up to beginners, a coach may want to simply have the novice player practice taking one step between these two points and shooting an imaginary ball. Then when the player has demonstrated he can do this well, add the ball and have the player practice with the ball. Lastly, because this shot is usually shot in heavy traffic, the shooter must concentrate on the target, which is the corner of the square on the backboard.

Every player on a team should be able to make jump-stop lay-ups and driving lay-ups from both sides of the floor with either hand. When compared to the jump shot and free throw, the lay-up is the easiest shot to master due to its proximity to the basket. However, the lay-up can be a difficult shot to make due to intense defensive pressure near the basket. Thus, a coach should utilize drills that will give his players confidence in shooting lay-ups under pressure.

The following drills can be implemented into a practice to develop different aspects of shooting the lay-up. However, the coach may need to modify the drills to fit his players needs and adjust the drills due to facility or equipment restrictions.

Lay-up Drills

The Two-Ball Lay-Up Drill

Objective: To condition and practice shooting.

Description: Have three players at each hoop with two basketballs. Place a basketball on each side of the lane on the low block. One player is a shooter who moves across the lane picking up the ball off the block and shoots a power lay-up. The other two players take up a position on each side of the lane. Their job is to rebound the shots that are shot on their side of the floor and place each ball back on the block so the ball is there for the shooter when he returns (Figures 5-1a and 5-1b). Time the drill for 30 seconds and then have the players rotate.

Coaching Points: Make sure that players shoot the ball with their right hand on the right side and their left hand on the left side. Also, the rebounders must place the ball on the block; do not let them bounce the ball to the shooter or pass the ball to the shooter. By making the shooter bend his knees to pick up the ball, he is practicing shooting the ball from a power position.

Figure 5-1a

Figure 5-1b

The Two-Ball Lay-Up Drill (with a shot fake)

Description: This drill is set up like the previous drill, but before the shooter shoots the ball he must give a strong pump fake.

Coaching Points: Make sure that on the pump fake the shooter does not shuffle his feet. Also, do not allow the shooter to make a pump fake from a standing position. He must be low! To make this drill even tougher, the coach can take a blocking pad and bump the shooter before he shoots.

The Power Lay-Up Off-the-Perimeter Drive Drill

Objective: To practice jump stopping off the dribble in the lane area and then shooting a power shot.

Description: Each player will have a ball and start at the free-throw line. Have the shooter execute a shot fake and then dribble drive with their right hand to the basket. The shooter should take no more than one dribble. After the hard dribble he must jump stop wherever he is in the lane and then jump straight up and shoot the ball. Time for 30 seconds and then have the players execute the drill by driving with their left hand, or move the players to a different spot on the perimeter.

Coaching Points: Make sure that on the shot fake the shooter does not come out of his stance or shuffle his feet. The shooter must also be reminded to drive directly to the hoop, i.e., the shooter should step in a straight line toward the baseline rather than stepping wide toward the sideline. Another shot fake can be added to this drill once the shooter jump stops in the lane. Encourage players not to fade on their shots.

The Lay-up Lines Drill

Description: Break the team up in to even numbers and put them on two sides of the court facing the basket. Place three to four balls in one of the lines. The line with the balls is the shooting line; the line without the balls is the rebounding line. Place the two lines about 20 feet from the basket and at an angle to the lane. Have the players practice driving in and shooting lay-ups from both sides of the court. Once a player shoots the ball he rotates over into the rebounding line and the rebounder rotates into the shooting line (Figure 5-2).

Coaching Points: Make sure the players are driving hard to the basket, are on balance, and are jumping off the proper leg. If a player is missing lay-ups, check the angle that he is attacking the basket. An adjustment the coach can make is to tell the shooter to attack the basket by running between the block and the first hash mark on the lane line. Also, make sure that the shooter is not staring at the ball as he is dribbling. This leads to poor concentration on the shot. Finally, make sure that on the right side of the court the players dribble and shoot with their right hand and on the left side they dribble and shoot with their left hand.

Figure 5-2

The Shot-Fake Lay-ups through Chairs Drill

Description: Break the players up into groups of three or four. Put each group at a basket and give each player a ball. Place two chairs at the free-throw line about four-feet apart. Have the first player in line at the top of the key. The drill begins by having the player toss the ball to himself and catch the ball on a jump stop. He will then shot fake and drive between the two chairs and go all the way to the basket and shoot a lay-up. Work for two minutes with the players driving with their right hand and then switch and have them drive and shoot with their left hand, or move the chairs to a different spot on the court and have them work from a new area.

Coaching Points: Do not allow the players to shuffle their feet when they start their drive. The players must take a positive step forward on their drive. A player may step back and then step forward and that is wasted movement and may negate any advantage that they get from their shot fake. The coach should have the players imagine that they are driving by a defender's body (Rick Pitino calls this *body-to-body*) when they step through the chairs. Tell the players to step directly to the basket and they should avoid stepping wide.

The Close-Out Shooting-to-Direct Drive Drill

Description: Put four players at a basket. Have three players on the baseline with a ball and one player at the top of the key. The player with the ball will throw a two-handed chest pass to the shooter at the top of the key. The passer will then execute a close out in an attempt to put pressure on the shooter. The shooter will shot fake on the defender and then drive to the hoop for a lay-up. The shooter will get his rebound and rotate to the line on the baseline and the defender will then become the shooter. The coach can do this drill for a specified time and then rotate the players to a new spot on the court.

Coaching Points: The footwork in this drill must be emphasized in the much same way as the previous drill. The coach may want the defenders to leap in the air and yell, "shot," as the shooter shot fakes. This will develop recognition in the shooter to react quickly and drive when he sees a defender leave his feet.

CHAPTER 6

Free Throws

For some players shooting a *free throw* is the single most difficult skill to master in the game. Ironically, it is in many ways the simplest thing to do. However, due to poor mechanics, some unusual physical quality—i.e., huge hands or lack of concentration—the free throw has become a bugaboo for many players. The following is the most basic breakdown of the free throw.

The first thing a player must be concerned with is body alignment. To make sure that his body is aligned correctly, the shooter should put the toe of his shooting foot at the center of the free-throw line. The center of the free-throw line is easy to find because of the nail in the center (this nail is used to mark the circle of the key when the court is painted; virtually every gym has this nail). It is imperative for the toe to be at the center of the free-throw line because this then aligns the ball with the center of the basket. His feet should be shoulder-width apart and his knees should be flexed. The elbow of his shooting hand should be directly underneath the ball in line with the knee of his shooting foot; his elbow should not be to the side or behind the ball (Figure 6-1). The index finger of his shooting hand is aligned with the air valve of the basketball. Once this is done, it ensures that the ball is in the center of the hoop and that the ball will not block the vision of the shooter as he releases the ball. Lastly, his head should be lined up over his belly button, and because his knees are flexed, the butt of the shooter should be sticking out a little bit.

The mechanics of shooting the ball require that the shooter start with his knees flexed and move upward as he releases the ball (Figure 6-2). The ball should rest on

Figure 6-1

the pad of his shooting hand about 8 to 10 inches from the body. The palm of his shooting hand should not touch the ball with the palm facing skyward. The shooter should have a wrinkle in his wrist when he is ready to shoot (Figure 6-3). His fingers are spread as wide as they can be, but comfortably.

The guide hand is on the side of the ball and is placed in such a way that the thumb of the guide hand and the thumb of the shooting hand form the letter T. On the release, the ball should roll over the tips of his four open fingers with his index finger being the last finger to touch the ball. After the release, the shooter should finish with a high follow-through with his shooting elbow above his ear and his fingers in the basket (sometimes called *hand in the cookie jar*). The shooter should not be falling in any direction after he finishes his shot. He should finish his shot by being on the balls of his feet, and if he does lose balance he should fall forward rather than backward. The key to being a good free-throw shooter is eliminating as much movement as possible. Thus, the shooter should not have extra motion in his free throw, such as wrapping the ball around his waist, excess dribbles, extra movement or hitches in the shot, etc.

The final element of shooting free throws is target and routine. The shooter has no right target to focus on when shooting. However, some targets are better than others. The best and most consistent target is the net attachment at the back of the rim. This

Figure 6-2

Figure 6-3

is a consistent target because every rim has the attachment, but more importantly, it is a target that is inside the rim. Some coaches say shoot at the front of the rim, or aim for the hole in the rim, or back rim. However, these targets sometimes require you to shoot past them to make the shot. It makes more sense to aim for the net attachment at the back of the rim because that is where the shooter wants the ball to go—in the rim. One other thing about the target is that no matter what it is, a player must keep his eye on it—i.e., he should not follow the flight of the ball. If a player follows the flight of the ball with his eyes, pretty soon his head starts to move and then his whole body is moving and he has lost his balance.

A player has many routines he could use and he has to figure out what works for him. The best advice is simple: Do what works and do it every time. Do not deviate. Just make sure that the routine does not add extra movement to the shot.

The following is a list of free throw drills that a coach can use throughout the season. A coach may want to chart when he uses these drills and try to determine which drills help his players the most. Or he may want to deviate from his usual free-throw routine and try something new. However, the one thing that a coach need to remember is that no matter what the drill, the players need to be focused when they shoot free throws, and they should shoot the ball the same way every time.

Free Throw Drills

- Match up pairs of players with opposite shooting percentages. Each man shoots 10 free throws—five or two at a time. Winners shower, losers are paired up for another challenge. Last man left must make two in a row before he showers.

- Seniors and juniors must each make one free throw or everyone must make two in a row.

- Entire team makes a certain number of total free throws or everyone must make two in a row.

- Coach versus the team captain.

- Group competition—lettermen versus non-lettermen.

- Make two in a row three times. Rotate after each two.

- Shoot 10, two at a time. Rotate and record.

- Shoot 20, five at a time. Rotate and record.

- Make 10, two at a time. Rotate and record.

- Make eight out of 10; shoot two at a time.

- Pick a player to make two in a row or everyone must perform a conditioning drill.

- Five minutes, shoot until a miss. The rebounder keeps track of most makes in a row.

- Shoot 40, ten at a time. Rotate and record. If a player makes 10 in a row, he can shower and record only up to that point. The 10 in a row must be in one series only.

- Ten minutes, shoot five at a time. Rotate and record.

- Everyone must make one in a row or the entire team must run a conditioning drill.

- Shoot for 10 minutes. Keep track of most shots made in a row. Record.

- Collectively, the team must make a set number within a prescribed number of attempts per player or everyone runs a conditioning drill. Repeat until the preset goal is reached.

- Run some type of a conditioning drill after each missed free throw in practice.

- First player to score five points at each basket can shower. Shoot two at a time. Points assigned as follows: swished free throw shot (+1); made shot that hits the rim (0); missed shot (−1). May also be employed as a two-, three-, or five-minute drill.

CHAPTER 7

Shooting

Shooting the basketball is the fun part of the game. It is something every player likes to do, but it is also the skill that is most often practiced and developed in the wrong way. Players then have a difficult time breaking these bad habits later.

Four Things that Make a Good Shooter

- *Correct form and technique*

Though it is very difficult for younger players to develop the correct form in its entirety, they should practice certain fundamentals repeatedly to develop muscle memory reflexes.

- *Hours of practice*

The correct technique does not do a player any good without many hours of practice. Ten minutes a day is not sufficient. Becoming a good shooter requires one to two hours of perfect practice every day, especially during the off-season.

- *The right mental approach*

The right mental approach includes understanding and concentrating on the correct techniques, staying out of the habit of missing, setting goals at every workout and practicing until those goals have been reached, relaxing and having fun, not getting discouraged, and sticking to a practice schedule. Players must make these commitments.

- *Accountability*

Players should make themselves accountable for each shot they take. They should know how many they make and how many they miss, and record their shots daily. They should not take shots and miss constantly, take shots they know are not *game shots*, or take shots they know they cannot make. It is easy for the brain to accept missing the basket; players should not allow themselves to get into this habit.

Correct Form and Technique

Every youngster has two major sources of power with which to shoot the ball: the arms and the legs. Using these sources of power in coordination with each other is very important in propelling the ball toward the basket. A player's strength, age, and size usually determine how much the arms and the legs must be used when shooting the basketball.

Younger, smaller players usually have to bend the knees deeply and lower the ball almost to their ankles to get it to the basket (Figures 7-1 through 7-3). These players are utilizing both sources of power available to them, which is the correct technique for shooting the basketball at their age. As players get older, stronger, and bigger, they will be able to focus on the other techniques of shooting and rely less on leg bend and arm movement.

Figure 7-1   Figure 7-2   Figure 7-3

The first step in shooting the basketball is to catch the ball or pick the ball up off the dribble in a bent-knee position. The legs supply the power, and in a sense, start the shot.

Stance

When preparing to shoot, the feet and shoulders should be squared to the basket (Figure 7-4). Although in game situations squaring up to the basket is not always possible, it is important that players square to the basket and use the proper techniques when practicing. The shooting foot should be slightly in front of the other. The ball should be held in the tuck position at or near the waist or chest.

Figure 7-4

Head

The head should remain still with the eyes on the target. Players should find a spot, whether it is the front or back of the rim or the entire basket, and focus on that spot for the entire shot. They should repeat this every single time, using the same spot. Players should not let the shooting arm and ball block their vision, making them a one-eyed shooter (Figure 7-5), but position themselves so they can focus on the target with both eyes (Figure 7-6).

It is acceptable for players to jump a bit on their shot, but they should not jump too much. They should not drift to one side or the other, jump inward, or fall back. This motion is unnecessary and will cause shooters to lose their balance and throw off their shot. When shooting the basketball, less body motion improves the shooter's chance of success. Players should land in relatively the same spot from which they took off, perhaps slightly forward.

Figure 7-5

Figure 7-6

Grip

The grip of the hands on the basketball is a crucial element of the shot. Kids should learn to be one-handed shooters rather than two-handed shooters. The index and middle fingers of the shooting hand, the ones which propels the ball, should be in the middle of the ball. The valve can be used as a guide. Players should position the valve between their index and middle finger and spread the other fingers out evenly on the ball (Figure 7-7). This technique will ensure that their hand is in the middle of the ball, creating a good balanced grip. If players can see their little finger on the ball, their grip is wrong; shooters should *hide the pinkie*.

The widest distance between fingers on the ball is between the thumb and the index finger. The ball should rest not in the palm of the shooting hand, but on the pads of the hands between the fingers and the palm. There should be enough space between the shooting hand and the ball to allow the coach to slip a pencil between the ball and the palm (Figure 7-8).

Figure 7-7

Figure 7-8

The non-shooting hand is referred to as the off hand, guide hand, or balance hand. Shooting is essentially a one-handed act. Shooters should not use the off hand to propel the ball, but simply to balance it. The fingers of the guide hand should point to the ceiling. The thumb of the guide hand should point to the shooter's ear. The thumbs should form a T on the basketball, but should not be touching each other (Figure 7-9).

Most basketball coaches would agree on specific fundamentals to gripping the basketball. Most experts would also agree on the differences that every coach teaches and advocates. Adjustments also have to be made for players who are smaller, weaker, or have small hands. Making these adjustments is an important part of a coach's job.

When picking the ball up off the dribble, players should be sure to get the proper grip to shoot. Their hands must slide to these positions automatically. Repetition is the only way to ensure this action. Players can flip the ball from hand to hand and practice catching it with the proper grip even when they are not at practice or on a basketball court.

Figure 7-9

Figure 7-10

The Release

As a player brings the basketball up to shoot, the ball should be placed above his right eye (for a right-handed shooter) just outside of his head, allowing both eyes to see the target. His elbow keeps the ball straight and it should be tucked to the side and pointed at the basket. His upper arm should be parallel to the floor, with his forearm perpendicular to the floor (Figure 7-10).

The player's arm should form the letter *L* under the ball (Figure 7-11). The ball should rest over his elbow, and his elbow should be over his shooting foot. His guide-hand elbow should be outside of his back foot. The wrist of his shooting hand should be cocked (flexed). If the wrist is cocked properly, the shooter will see wrinkles in his wrist. The release of the shot is extremely important. The initial movement to start the shot is upward. Players should remember to push the ball up, not out. If the release is properly executed, their elbow will end up higher than their chin (Figure 7-12).

Figure 7-11

Figure 7-12

The top of the wrist should be as high as or higher than the backboard. The shot rolls off the player's index and middle fingers. These two fingers should be the last things to touch the basketball. This technique puts the proper backspin on the ball, creating a softness to the shot. His off hand should come off the ball quickly, with his fingers pointing to the ceiling and his thumb to his ear (Figure 7-13).

Follow-Through

On the follow-through, the fingers of the shooting hand should appear to be cupped slightly over the rim, not pointing to the floor (Figures 7-14 and 7-15). Some coaches use the phrase "Pose for the picture" to remind shooters of this technique.

The arc on the shot is based on several factors, including the shooter's distance from the basket, the use of the backboard, and what is comfortable for the shooter. With too much arc, the shooter may be expending too much energy. Without enough arc, the shot will be too flat. When a shooter is using the backboard on a shot, the ball should be shot higher and softer. An uncoordinated follow-through or no follow-through at all violates the rules of good shooting.

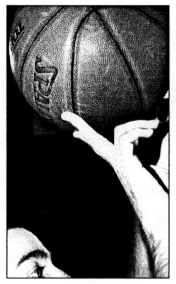

Figure 7-13   Figure 7-14   Figure 7-15

Rules of Good Shooting

- The body should remain relatively still.
- The shot should be smooth and balanced.
- The shooter should concentrate on the proper techniques.
- The shooter should *pose for the picture* on the follow-through.

Summary of the Techniques of Shooting

One of a coach's responsibilities is to correct poor techniques and help players progress. To fulfill this responsibility, coaches should be aware of the correct techniques and watch the players closely. The shooting checklist on the next page summarizes the techniques of good shooting. Coaches and players should use this list to evaluate a player's development. Videotaping a player's shot for the coach and player to watch together can be very helpful in this evaluation.

Developing Correct Shooting

Warm Up Properly

Coaches should have one ball for every player. Girls and smaller boys can use a girl's ball. Very young players should use a junior-sized ball. Players should learn with a ball that is appropriate for their size.

Needs Work	Triple-Threat Position	Needs Work	The Actual Shot and Finish
			1. Elbow and Arm
☐	1. Tuck ball	☐	—elbow tucked to side—pointed at hoop
☐	2. Starting blocks—knees bent	☐	—upper arm parallel to floor
☐	3. Ball fakes	☐	—forearm perpendicular to floor
☐	4. Ball quick	☐	—ball over elbow, elbow over shooting foot
☐	5. Body-to-body drives	☐	—guide-hand elbow—outside of foot
Needs Work	**Set Up**		**2. Wrist**
☐	1. Knees bent	☐	—cocked (flexed)—see wrinkles
☐	2. 1-2 step approach off pass		**3. Release**
☐	3. Squared to basket	☐	—extension of arm—push out
☐	4. Off dribble-plant inside foot	☐	—roll ball off index and middle finger—backspin
Needs Work	**Head and Eyes**	☐	—follow through: wrist as high or higher than backboard; fingers cupped over rim; fingers not pointed to floor; pose for picture at least one second
☐	1. Head still		
☐	2. Both eyes on target		
☐	3. Don't follow flight of ball	☐	—follow-through: guide hand gets off ball quickly; fingers of guide hand point to ceiling
Needs Work	**The Grip**		**4. Jump**
	1. Shooting Hand	☐	—land in relatively same spot as left the floor from
☐	—hand on the ball, fingers spread		
☐	—ball on pads		
☐	—hand in middle of ball		
	2. Guide Hand/Balance Hand		
☐	—fingers pointing to ceiling		
☐	—thumb to ear		
☐	—both thumbs form T		
Overall Evaluation			

Figure 7-16. Shooting checklist

The On-Your-Back Shooting Drill

Description: This drill may be performed without a basket or a court. Players lie on their backs on the floor with the ball in their shooting hand. They *shoot* the ball using their normal shooting movement, keeping their elbow close to their body and the seams of the ball horizontal. This positioning helps create backspin on the shot, but most important, it helps players work on their follow-through. As players shoot, they should keep the follow-through position until just before the ball hits their wrist on its way down (Figure 7-17).

Coaching Points: It is easy for players to evaluate themselves when executing this drill. If the ball returns straight to the palm of the hand after the *shot*, the shot was made. If it does not, the shot was missed.

The Chair Drill

Objective: To work on getting power from the arms, putting the proper arc on the shot, aligning the elbow correctly, and following through.

Description: The coach should place a chair five to eight feet in front of the basket, depending on the size and strength of the players. The first player sits on the chair. The player must then use his arms—not his legs—to propel the ball upward to the basket (Figure 7-18). Players—particularly smaller ones—must start the ball head high and with one rhythmic motion, rotate their arm down to their waist and then back into shooting position to shoot the ball up at the basket. Again, this chair drill forces players to get their arms into the shot.

Figure 7-17

Figure 7-18

Drills to Improve Techniques

To develop the right grip and follow-through techniques, the coach can wrap a piece of white adhesive tape around the center of the basketball. Players grip the ball with their index and middle fingers straddling the tape. If the players use the correct techniques when shooting, the ball should go toward the basket with proper backspin and the tape on the basketball should rotate symmetrically (Figures 7-19 and 7-20). If the tape *wobbles* or does not rotate at all, then the players have a flaw in their grip, their release, or their follow-through.

Another drill helps players grip the ball properly as well as get into proper triple-threat position. Players toss the ball five to six feet in front of them with backspin, then run up and catch it off the bounce, quickly adjusting their hands to the tape on the ball to ensure the proper grip. After catching the ball, players get into triple-threat position and work on rocker steps, fakes, and pivots.

Next, players toss the ball out in front of them, catch it on a balanced jump stop, grip it properly, and take a shot. Players can judge their techniques by watching the rotation of the tape on the ball on its way to the basket. These *tape-on-the-ball* drills can be used to emphasize the three S's:

- Spin (backspin)
- Stop (players should stop on balance and be squared to the basket)
- Sight

While performing drills, coaches should instruct players to work quickly, but not rush themselves. Young kids tend to do things in a hurry. In basketball, this tendency causes players to be off-balance and out of control.

Shooting Off the Dribble

When shooting off the dribble, players should escape their defender and get a good look at the basket. If a defender is close enough to the ball handler to get a hand in and distract the shooter, the offensive player should not be looking to shoot. When closely guarded, offensive players should look to drive or pass. When players are within their shooting range and are not closely guarded, they should look to shoot or pass. When shooting off the dribble, players should use the following techniques:

- After getting by the defender, players should come to a jump stop off a hard dribble by planting their inside foot (the one closest to the basket), and swinging their other foot to square to the basket and gain balance. The last dribble before going into the shot should be slightly lower and harder than the others. This gives shooters some momentum as they prepare to jump into the shot.

- Their knees should stay bent as the players come to a jump stop.
- While squared to the basket, players should begin their shot using correct form and technique (Figure 7-21).

It is important that each player be able to effectively handle the basketball. Players who cannot handle the basketball and escape their defender to get a good shot are very limited in their ability to help their team. Players should work on their ball handling skills daily; these skills can be practiced without a basket or a court.

Figure 7-19

Figure 7-20

Figure 7-21

Shooting-Off-the-Dribble Drills

Drill #1

Description: Players should form a line at the wing position. Players drive to the middle using two dribbles and take a shot from the free-throw line area (Figure 7-22).

Drill #2

Description: Players form a line at the top of the key. Players fake right and drive left using one or two dribbles, then shoot. On the second repetition of the drill, players fake left and drive right.

Coaching Points: Coaches should pay close attention to the players' techniques during these drills and make corrections when necessary. Above all, coaches should make sure that players cover from four to six feet with every dribble of the basketball. Too often, players bounce the ball and cover only 6 to 12 inches of the floor space.

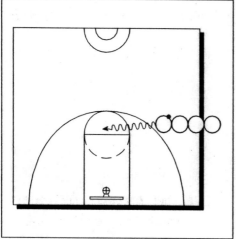

Figure 7-22

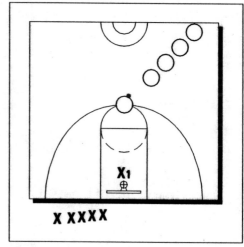

Figure 7-23

Shooting-Under-Pressure Drills

The Under-Pressure Drill

Description: The players are aligned as shown in Figure 7-23, with one defender (X) positioned under the basket and one offensive player (O) at the top of the key. The defender passes out to the offensive player. Offensive players should use a one- to two-step approach to catch the ball and begin their shot. Defenders rush out at the offensive players and try to distract them as they shoot. The defender is not allowed to touch the ball or the shooter. After the shot is taken, the players go to the end of the opposite line.

Coaching Point: Coaches should emphasize to their players that good shooters do not allow themselves to be distracted by the defense.

The Distract-the-Player Drill

Description: This drill involves several important basketball techniques. The players are aligned around the arc as shown in Figure 7-24. The distance from the basket may be adjusted for younger players. X1, the defender, passes the ball out to O7, then rushes out to distract him. The defender is not allowed to touch the ball or the shooter. After O7 shoots the ball, X1 takes his place. O7 retrieves the ball whether the shot was made or missed and shoots a lay-up. Shooters can earn up to three points. They earn two for a made outside shot and one for a successful lay-up. If the defender touches the ball or the shooter, the shooter is automatically awarded three points and can earn a fourth by making the lay-up. After shooting the lay-up, O7 becomes the defensive player and passes the ball out to the next shooter, O6 in the diagram. The process continues around the arc for a designated number of repetitions, and the player with the most points is the winner.

Coaching Points:

- Good shooting is a matter of concentrating and not being distracted by the defender.
- Good defense on shooters mean distracting the shooters and breaking their concentration without fouling.
- Making open shots, particularly lay-ups, is the key to winning offensive basketball.
- Getting a shot off quickly after receiving a pass is another key to good shooting. The coach should emphasize receiving the ball in a bent-knee position, while stepping toward the pass, using a one- to two-step approach to the incoming pass.
- The coach should not allow the defender to make poor passes to the offensive player. Passers should make a crisp, two-handed chest pass to the shooter. If the pass does not arrive at the receiver's chest, the pass should be made again.

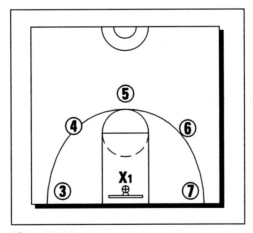

Figure 7-24

What Is a Bad Shot?

Coaches should teach their players more than basketball techniques and skills; they should also teach them basketball principles and philosophy. When teaching shooting, coaches should explain to players the difference between a good shot and a bad shot. Good shots and bad shots may vary from player to player, but the determination is always made according to the same rules.

A Bad Shot Is ...

- A shot at which the player is not proficient.
- A shot taken when the player is off-balance.
- A shot taken when the defense has a hand in the player's face.
- A shot that the player is forced to change in midair.
- A shot that does not come within the framework of the offense.
- A shot taken but never practiced in practice situations.
- A shot taken when fatigued.
- A shot taken when the player is not in shot rhythm (for example, when the player fumbled the ball or stumbled).
- A shot taken when a teammate has a better shot and is open.
- A shot taken without considering the game situation or time element.
- A shot taken when a player has just come off the bench and is not in the flow of the game.
- A shot taken when no teammates are ready to rebound.

Mental Aspects of Shooting

Besides the physical techniques, good shooting includes many mental aspects. To make their players into good shooters, coaches should also address these factors.

Coaches should motivate players to practice on their own. One way to improve players' motivation is to help them create a good self-image. Coaches should not simply berate a player for missing or taking a poor shot. Instead, they should explain to the player why the shot was missed (the errors in technique or form) or why the shot was a poor shot.

Coaches should also help players set realistic shooting goals. These goals will vary depending on the age and ability of the player. For example, a player's goal might be to shoot 50 lay-ups three times a week, to never be short with a shot, or to make three straight shots from a specific spot in practice before moving to a different area.

It is also important for coaches to help their players visualize when shooting. They can tell players about the size of the rim, that it is big enough for three balls to fit into it at the same time (Figure 7-25). Showing players how big the rim is can increase their confidence in their ability to make a basket. Coaches might also tell players to visualize the ball going over the rim and the net swishing as the shot goes through it (Figure 7-26), or to imagine a target on the rim (Figure 7-27). By helping players to relax and use various visualization exercises, coaches can make youngsters better shooters.

To become an effective player and a great shooter, players should be able to make a greater percentage of shots than ever before. When no one is guarding them, they should be able to hit 60 to 70 percent of their shots in practice depending on their age. They should learn to shoot properly even when they are tired and their concentration begins to waver. They should also have a shooting spot, a favorite area on the floor from which they know they can always make a shot, and a bread-and-butter shot — a favorite shot they know they can always make. Finally, they should learn to concentrate. They should be able to hit six to eight shots in a row. Ideally, when players are practicing without anyone guarding them, they should never miss more than three shots in a row.

Figure 7-25

Figure 7-26

Figure 7-27

The Eight-Minute Drill

Description: Players should shoot 50 to 100 shots from a particular spot without stopping. They should be able to shoot the 100 shots in about eight minutes. To really work hard, players should shoot, retrieve their own rebound, and dribble back out to their spot. This drill should be performed at least three times a week. It is easy for players to cheat or slack off, but they are only hurting themselves. If players are committed to becoming great shooters, they will take the drill seriously.

Coaching Points: Players could have a partner to chart their shots. The chart should have the numbers 1 through 100 written on it in order. If the shot is missed, the partner puts a slash through the number. If the shot is made, the partner circles the number. Players can then total their field goal percentage, most consecutive made shots, and most consecutive missed shots. Refer to Figure 7-28 for a sample shooting chart.

What Makes a Good Shooter?

1. Correct form and technique
2. Countless hours of practice

3. Having the right mental approach
4. Accountability

Date _____

FGA _____ FGM _____

Consecutive makes _____

Consecutive misses _____

1	2	3	4	5	6	7	8	9	10	11	12	13	14	15
16	17	18	19	20	21	22	23	24	25	26	27	28	29	30
31	32	33	34	35	36	37	38	39	40	41	42	43	44	45
46	47	48	49	50	51	52	53	54	55	56	57	58	59	60
61	62	63	64	65	66	67	68	69	70	71	72	73	74	75
76	77	78	79	80	81	82	83	84	85	86	87	88	89	90
91	92	93	94	95	96	97	98	99	100					

Date _____

FGA _____ FGM _____

Consecutive makes _____

Consecutive misses _____

1	2	3	4	5	6	7	8	9	10	11	12	13	14	15
16	17	18	19	20	21	22	23	24	25	26	27	28	29	30
31	32	33	34	35	36	37	38	39	40	41	42	43	44	45
46	47	48	49	50	51	52	53	54	55	56	57	58	59	60
61	62	63	64	65	66	67	68	69	70	71	72	73	74	75
76	77	78	79	80	81	82	83	84	85	86	87	88	89	90
91	92	93	94	95	96	97	98	99	100					

Date _____

FGA _____ FGM _____

Consecutive makes _____

Consecutive misses _____

1	2	3	4	5	6	7	8	9	10	11	12	13	14	15
16	17	18	19	20	21	22	23	24	25	26	27	28	29	30
31	32	33	34	35	36	37	38	39	40	41	42	43	44	45
46	47	48	49	50	51	52	53	54	55	56	57	58	59	60
61	62	63	64	65	66	67	68	69	70	71	72	73	74	75
76	77	78	79	80	81	82	83	84	85	86	87	88	89	90
91	92	93	94	95	96	97	98	99	100					

For Free Throw Concentration:

The Perfect Free Throw: **One which swishes or hits back part of rim and comes right back to the shooter**

Recording Free Throws: **The perfect free throw** ●

Made but not perfect ╱

Missed free throw ○

Figure 7-28.

Individual Shooting Practice

Coaches use drills in practice to teach shooting. Players should also practice on their own. They can use several drills when practicing alone to improve their shot.

The Spot-Shooting-Versus-the-Pro Drill

Description: Players should pick a spot and take 25 shots from that spot. They should then take 25 shots from the spot off one hard dribble; 25 shots off two hard dribbles; and 25 shots after a good head, ball, and foot fake. They should keep track of the number of shots made and award themselves one point for every shot they make. Michael Jordan is awarded two points for every shot they miss (Figure 7-29).

Sample Chart			
Date	**Shots Taken**	**My Score**	**Michael Jordan's Score**
June 2	100	60	80
June 3	50	35	30
June 4	100	55	90
June 5	100	71	58

Figure 7-29. Sample scoring chart

On June 2, for example, the player made 60 shots for 60 points. The player missed 40 shots, so Jordan was given 80 points. To win, players must make 67 percent of their shots.

The Zero-Backwards Drill

Description: Players pick one or more spots to shoot from and choose a number (six, for example) to start with. They subtract one for every shot they make and add one for every shot they miss. They should practice until they reach zero.

The Form-Concentration Drill

Description: Using the basketball shooting checklist, players should choose one of the techniques to emphasize. For example, a player may focus on keeping the elbow tucked in, positioning of the wrist on the follow-through, or releasing the ball properly. The players then check that point on every shot they take.

The Time-Yourself Drill

Description: Players should shoot consecutive shots for 5 or 10 minutes, keeping track of how many they make or miss. Their goal should be to make 65 percent of their shots. Players should keep their practice goals high because shooting percentages always drop during game competition. If players cannot make 50 percent of their shots in practice, they will certainly not shoot well when someone is guarding them. Again, age will determine these percentage goals.

Videotape Yourself

Players should ask someone to videotape their shooting and then go over the video with the help of their shooting checklist. Players should watch the video in slow motion and critique themselves on each point: triple-threat position, the set up, the head and eyes, the grip, the shot, and the finish. By studying themselves on tape, players will learn to analyze their shot and correct problems.

Becoming Familiar With the Basketball

Players should place a strip of tape around the center of the ball. At times when they are not practicing, they can condition their hands and fingers to grip the ball correctly by tossing the ball 6 to 12 inches in the air and catching it with their index and middle fingers straddling the tape.

Common Mistakes in Shooting the Basketball

Teaching young players the art of shooting the basketball can be an overwhelming task. Before beginning, coaches should be aware of the following mistakes commonly made by youngsters:

- Smaller or weaker players often do not get their arms into the shot. They bend their legs, but put the ball up too quickly with their arms. Their arms and legs are both sources of power, and should work together.
- Young players often put the wrong foot forward. Right-handed shooters should have their right foot slightly in front of their left. Left-handed shooters should have their left foot slightly in front of their right.
- The player's shoulders are not square to the basket.
- The player's eyes follow the shot while it is in the air, snapping his head backward. This motion causes a jerk in the release.
- The player's wrist is not cocked, and the ball is pushed outward or slung toward the basket rather than being pushed upward. The same problem occurs if his elbow is not pointed at the basket.

- The player's arm is not straight at the conclusion of the shot, nor is his wrist bent on the follow-through.
- The player shoots without bending his legs. If his legs are not bent, they do not supply any power to the shot.
- Players do not release the shot quickly enough. They spend too much time aiming, often *measuring* their shot. As a result of this slow release, their shot is blocked.

When players shoot the basketball, there should be little or no movement of their head. Snapping their head back, swinging their shoulders to the side, and shuffling their feet should all be avoided. These actions do nothing but destroy the smoothness and consistency of the shot.

Once players understand the proper techniques, the key element is repetition. To be consistently good shooters, players must repeatedly practice shooting properly. This repetition is especially important for free throws.

Concentration and mental discipline are critical to good shooting. Players cannot allow the defense to distract them, and they must also learn to fight fatigue, game pressure, the crowd, and themselves. Mental discipline is especially important in free-throw shooting. Players should not be allowed to talk while shooting free throws in practice. It is also important for coaches to help their players develop confidence and a positive mental attitude when it comes to shooting. A combination of enthusiasm, hard work, and goal setting equals success.

CHAPTER 8

Coordination and Conditioning Drills

During initial practices, coaches will notice that their athletes are at different athletic levels and varying degrees of physical shape. Because of this, they will want to incorporate drills into each practice that can develop physical condition and coordination in all their players. By showing their players how to do coordination drills in practice, it should inspire the fledgling basketball player to work on these drills at home to further aid in the development of the athlete and the entire team.

The following drills and exercises can be used to develop agility, coordination, conditioning, and quickness in the athlete. They should be performed several times a week to be effective. Coaches should pick and choose the ones they feel will be the most beneficial in their practices.

The Small Hurdle or Cone Drills

Equipment Needed: The coach should place 5 to 12 hurdles or cones two- to three-feet apart. Hurdles actually work best for these drills because it is easier for players to cheat with cones. If the coach doesn't have access to real hurdles, he can make small hurdles by taking two cones and attaching a wood strip across the top. Another option for coaches is to actually make small hurdles out of plywood. Using two pieces of wood, the coach can attach one piece of wood to a base to form an upside-down T, or cut a groove into the base to insert the upright board into it. The hurdles should be between 8 and 12 inches high depending on the age of the players. The coach can have the players run several drills using the hurdles or cones.

Description:

- Players weave in and out of the hurdles in figure-eight fashion as quickly as they can.
- Players jump off both feet over the hurdles. This drill helps them learn to maintain their balance.
- Players pick up their right leg and jump over the hurdles with their left leg. This drill helps them learn to maintain their balance. After a designated number of repetitions, the players pick up their left leg and jump over the hurdles with their right leg.
- Players run the hurdle course and jump over the hurdles without stopping (Figure 8-1).
- Players alternate jumping off the right foot and jumping off both feet. After a specified number of repetitions, players alternate jumping off the left foot and jumping off both feet.
- Players repeat all of the previous drills while holding a basketball at chest level.
- Players repeat the first five drills while holding a basketball above their head with their arms straight up and elbows locked (Figure 8-2).

Figure 8-1

Figure 8-2

- Players repeat the first five drills with a two- to three-pound barbell weight in each hand.
- Players jump over the hurdles while a coach throws a basketball to them (Figure 8-3).

It is important to emphasize that jumping drills are not to be done on concrete or tile surfaces. Injuries to knees can occur more frequently on concrete or tile as opposed to grassy or wooden surfaces.

Figure 8-3

The Stop-and-Go Running Drill

Description: This exercise can be run using a basketball court or any 15- to 20-yard straightaway. On the coach's whistle, players sprint until the whistle is blown again, then make a balanced stop, stay low, turn the other way, and sprint in that direction until the next whistle.

Coaching Points: The coach should make the sprints different lengths to keep the players from anticipating the whistle. The players should stay low and pivot quickly. The coach can gradually increase the duration of the drill.

The Slides-with-Hand/Eye-Coordination Dril

Equipment Needed: This drill requires three small objects that can be picked up and carried while sliding, such as blocks of treated wood or similar items.

Description: The coach should place two of these blocks 15–to 20-feet apart. Players hold the third block in their hand. They should maintain a good defensive stance and slide to one of the blocks on the floor, put their block down and pick up the one from the floor, and slide the other direction, repeating the process (Figures 8-4 and 8-5). This drill should initially be run for 30 seconds and gradually increased to two minutes. The goal for repetitions should be adjusted based on the age of the players.

Figure 8-4

Figure 8-5

Jump Rope

Equipment Needed: A jump rope, which is a valuable tool for helping athletes develop and maintain coordination.

Description: When players jump rope, they should not turn the rope by making big sweeping motions with their arms. Instead, they should keep their hands at their waist and turn their wrists to keep the rope going.

The Tire Drill

Description: This drill is similar to the small hurdles drill. Players jump in and out of a tire, jumping with the right foot, left foot, or both feet.

The Tire Run Drill

Description: The coach should position 5 to 12 tires in a line. The players should run quickly down the line, placing one foot in the tires. They should concentrate on keeping their balance and coordination.

The Four-Square Tire Drill

Description: The coach should place four tires in a square. Players jump from tire to tire around the square, using the right foot, left foot, and both feet.

The Run-in-Place Drill

Description: This drill is also called the fast-feet drill. Players should get in a good stance with their feet slightly wider than their shoulders and run in place as quickly as they can. This drill should initially be run for 30 seconds and gradually increased to two or three minutes.

Coaching Points: The coach should also add quick quarter turns to the left and right. These turns should be done on the coach's whistle, with the players making the quick turn and then returning to their original position and continuing the drill.

The Wall/Basket Tipping Drill

Description: Players should stand in front of a wall or basket, throw the ball off the wall or backboard, and work on tipping the ball with one hand (Figure 8-6). Players should work with both the left hand and the right hand. When tipping, the arm should be fully extended and locked at the elbow. The player should use a quick flick of the wrist to tip the ball, land in a balanced position, and go back up to tip the ball again. Players should try to continue tipping the ball for a designated period of time without making a mistake.

The All-Fours Drill

Objective: To improve agility, coordination, and quickness.

Description: Players should get down on all fours in a good, low four-point football stance. They should slide back and forth between two designated spots on the floor as quickly as possible (Figure 8-7).

The Cut-and-Go Drill

Description: The coach marks the floor with taped X's at various spots. Beginning at one baseline, the players run the length of the floor. They should hit the X with their outside foot, plant their foot, and push off it for a quick change of direction (Figure 8-8). Performing this drill correctly requires concentration and coordination.

Coaching Point: The coaches should focus on timing and coordination rather than speed during this drill.

The Diagonal Rope Drill

Equipment Needed: A 15- to 20-foot rope

Description: The coach should attach the rope to a wall or door at a height of four feet and anchor the other end to the floor. Players should stand with one side to the rope and, using a two-footed take off, jump quickly from side to side over the rope (Figure 8-9). They continue to progress up the rope until they do not think they can jump any higher, then turn around and jump backwards down the rope to the starting point, repeating for 30 seconds.

Figure 8-6

Figure 8-7

Figure 8-8

Figure 8-9

Body Obstacle Race

Objective: To increase foot agility, coordination, and quickness in reaction.

Description: The squad is divided into two equal teams. The players lie prone on their backs or on their stomachs in two straight lines as indicated in Figure 8-10. When the drill is run for the first time, the players should be five- to six-feet apart. The relay race

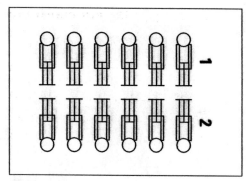

Figure 8-10

begins with the first player in each line running and jumping over the players who lie prone on their backs. When the players reach the last player on the floor, they turn around and jump over their teammates again until they reach their original positions. When they reach their original positions they lie back down on the floor and yell, "go," which signals the next player in line to repeat the same procedure. The winner is the first team to have all players complete the relay.

Coaching Points: Coaches can vary this drill by increasing or decreasing the distance between players on the floor, making it more difficult to time the jumps properly. They can also require players to use a pull-up jump, taking off from both feet, or run backward over the prone players. All of these variations help increase foot coordination and agility, as well as provide a fun activity for the players.

Players have so many skills and techniques to learn that running alone is not the most efficient use of a coach's limited practice time. Coaches should search for drills that combine conditioning with important basketball skills. The following drills, for example, can be run either as explained or while dribbling a basketball.

Sideline Sprints

Description: The players line up on one sideline and sprint back and forth from sideline to sideline. The goal is to be able to cross the court 14 to 16 times in one minute.

Full-Court Sprints

Description: This drill is similar to the sideline sprints, but the players line up on one baseline and sprint the length of the court. The goal is to run the length of the court 9 to 10 times in one minute.

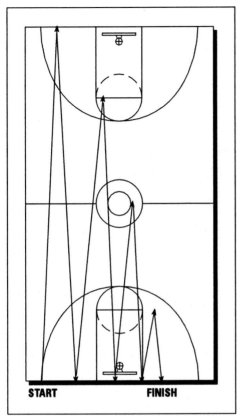

Figure 8-11

START   FINISH

The Stop-and-Go Drill

Description: The kids begin sprinting as hard as they can. When the coach blows the whistle, they stop and begin sprinting in the opposite direction. This continues for 30 seconds to one minute.

The Defensive Slides Drill

Description: Players line up at one elbow of the free-throw lane and slide back and forth from elbow to elbow for 30 seconds.

The Single-Line Touch Drill

Description: All coaches run some variation of this drill. The players start at one baseline. They run and touch the opposite baseline and return to the start, run and touch the opposite free-throw line and return to the start, run and touch the 10-second line and return to the start, and run and touch the near free-throw line and return to the start (Figure 8-11).

Coaching Point: The coach may vary the drill by requiring the players to run with their arms raised above their shoulders.

The Double-Line Touch Drill

Description: This drill is run in the same manner as the single-line touch drill except that the players run and touch each line twice before moving on to the next one.

Distance Conditioning

Youngsters who are determined to be good basketball players should continue to practice during the off-season. Distance running is a good way for players to stay in shape. The following three programs are recommended for players to use in the off-season or on their own time during the season. Coaches will usually not have time to implement them in their normal practice schedules. It is important to realize that adjustments have to be made for each drill depending on the age and physical maturity level of the players.

Program 1—Cross Country Running

Description: This program involves 30 minutes of running or jogging anywhere. The player runs until fatigued, walks until rested, and runs again. The player continues to run and walk for 30 minutes.

Program 2—Lap Program

Description: A football field works best for this program. Players sprint 40 yards, walk the next 10 yards, and sprint the next 40 yards. They then run backward around the goalpost and end zone and repeat the process on the other side of the field. After completing one lap around the field, the players rest for 30 seconds, then run another lap. Players should try to start out with three or four laps around the field and gradually increase the total number of laps.

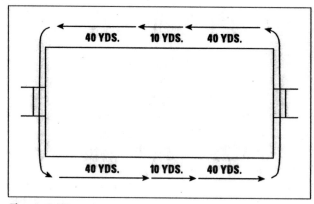

Figure 8-12

Program 3—Sprint Program

Description: Players should run 10 40-yard sprints, with a 15-second rest after each one. They should run each sprint as hard as they can. If it is possible to time them, their goal should be to be between 5.0 and 5.9 seconds for each sprint. This goal may vary based on players' ages and conditioning levels.

CHAPTER 9

Tips for Coaches

The different types of basketball coaches vary as much as the different levels of basketball. Coaches range from highly paid professionals to volunteers, from veteran former players to novices who have never taken a jump shot. Each coach has taken on a formidable task. This responsibility is perhaps most intimidating at the youth level, where coaches are often expected to teach their players the fundamentals of basketball while having a significant impact on the children's lives. This job is especially difficult for those parents who accepted a coaching position so their children would have the opportunity to play, but know little or nothing about the game of basketball, and even less about coaching it.

Coaches should consider several questions before their first practice. What skills are important for their players to learn, and what is the best way to teach them? How can they maximize their practice time? How do they set up a practice schedule? What if during certain times no gym is available for practice? Should they play to win or let the kids play for fun? These are important considerations for the youth basketball coach that will be addressed in this chapter.

The youth coach's job primarily involves teaching. Teaching does not take place on its own; it is an art. The four basic steps of the learning process are explanation, demonstration, imitation, and repetition.

Explanation

The first step in teaching is *explanation*. Coaches should explain to their players what they want them to learn and use terminology the children can understand. It is also important for coaches to remember that children have short attention spans and tailor their explanations accordingly.

Demonstration

The second step in teaching is *demonstration*. After explaining the skill they want to teach, coaches should demonstrate it for their players. Coaches have several ways to accomplish this step. If they are comfortable performing the skill, they can demonstrate it themselves. If not, they can ask someone else to come to practice or use one of their players to demonstrate the skill, or use a videotape.

Imitation

The third step in teaching is called *imitation*. After demonstrating the skill, coaches should give players the opportunity to practice it themselves. During this step, it is important that the players practice performing the skill correctly. Coaches should observe the players carefully and make corrections when necessary.

Repetition

The final step in the learning process is *repetition*. The players should practice the skill regularly to become familiar with it. Drills and games can be used to keep that practice from becoming monotonous.

Coaches who have never played basketball must be creative when it comes to teaching their players certain skills and techniques. They can show portions of instructional videos to the children and point out the correct techniques. They can also ask a friend or another parent for assistance. If they have players who are skilled in certain techniques, they can use those players to demonstrate for the rest of the team.

It is also difficult for these coaches to observe each player's techniques during practice, especially if they are the only coach for 10 or 12 players. Because bad habits are hard to break, it is important that children learn good habits early. One way for coaches to observe all their players is to videotape a practice or a game. They can then watch the tape either alone or with their players, looking for proper technique. If they watch the tape with their players, coaches should be extremely careful in their praise and criticism of individual players.

Coaches should remember that kids will not catch on to a new skill right away, nor will they all learn at the same rate. It will take several practices before most of them are familiar with a skill, and some kids may never really become comfortable with it. Basketball is a difficult game for kids to play. It can also be intimidating. The proximity of the fans and the low number of players on the court at a time tend to expose players who have difficulty with such fundamentals as dribbling, passing and catching, or shooting, and can make these players feel inadequate or embarrassed. Helping players to have fun and building their self-esteem is another important responsibility of youth coaches.

Simple diagrams can be very helpful in explaining plays to kids. To avoid confusion, coaches should be consistent whenever they use basketball terminology or diagram symbols. Figure 9-1 illustrates common terms for different areas of the basketball court.

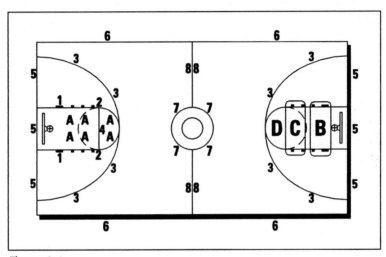

Figure 9-1

The following symbols are standard when diagramming basketball plays:

1—Block
2—Elbow
3—Three-point line
4—Foul line
5—End line/baseline
6—Sideline

7—Center jump circle
8—Mid court/one-half line/10-second line
A—Three-second area/multipurpose area/paint/key
B—Low post
C—Midpost
D—High post

Offensive player— **0**
Defensive player— **X**
Ball/cone— ● △

Movement of a player without the ball— ————
Movement of a player dribbling the ball— ∼∼∼
Movement of a player to set a screen— ————|
Movement of the ball via a pass— - - - - - - -

Considerations before Structuring a Practice

Before a coach can structure a practice, he has to take into consideration six variables: time, facilities, equipment, assistance, a player's skill level, and safety.

Time

Time considerations are vital, and a coach must know exactly how much time he will be allotted to work with his players. For instance, if a coach is only meeting with his team for one hour once a week, then he needs to structure each practice with a focus on one or two fundamentals. Then each subsequent practice needs a quick review of the previous week's fundamentals and an introduction of one or two new fundamentals. This structure would continue throughout the season, so that by the end the players have learned how to execute a number of fundamentals in both drills and games.

Facilities

A coach's knowledge of the *facilities* is essential in any practice planning. If a coach has 10 players and only half a court to work with, he is going to be severely limited with what he can do in terms of teaching game-time concepts. However, it should not hinder his ability to teach and drill many fundamentals. If a coach does have three or four baskets at his disposal, then he can structure his practices accordingly. For instance, he can have two to three players to a basket working on a particular shot, or he can have a station at each basket and rotate groups through each station.

Another facility issue is that other teams may be using the gym at the same time. This can prove to be a huge distraction to players of all ages. The coach must then incorporate ways of keeping kids' attention into his practices. One general rule is that he should not spend a lot of time talking; he should get the players moving. When the coach does need to talk to the players, then he should stand close to a wall with his back to it. This way the players have their back to the action and the only thing in their field of vision is the coach.

Equipment

In regards to *equipment*, it is simple—have lots of basketballs available. Each player should have a ball to work with and a coach should use basketballs that are the proper size for his players. Many leagues supply the properly sized basketballs.

Assistance or Assistants

If a team has two or three *assistant coaches*, then more fundamentals can be taught and practiced. The head coach should structure practice so that each coach works with a different group of kids.

Skills

The *skill level* of the players will determine how long drills are done, how fast, how often, and how complex. For instance, if a team has players with poor passing and catching skills, then the drills must be done very slowly to prevent injuries and build up confidence. On the other hand, if a team has players who can pass and catch consistently, then the coach must implement drills that will challenge the players, i.e., three-man weaves, two-ball passing, or the use of weighted balls.

One point that the coach should remember is that the poorer the players, the more scrimmaging that must be done in practice. Conversely, the more skilled the players, the more drill work that must be done. The rationale is that skilled players with basketball experience can usually synthesize how a drill carries over into a game situation. However, an unskilled player cannot understand the carry over from drill to game; the poorer players must scrimmage before they can see the use of a drill.

Safety

Never do any drill that would compromise the *safety* of the players. Make sure courts are dry and swept free of debris. Also make sure that the players are properly outfitted and always schedule water breaks into the practice plan. A coach should always have access to a phone and a well-stocked first aid kit at every practice.

What to Do in Practice

No matter how long a practice is, it should be broken down into segments that focus on *explaining skills, demonstrating skills, correcting skills,* and then *repeating skills.* Correct repetition of the skill is vital to the development of the player, but a balance coexists between introducing a new skill and repeating an old one. Once a skill has been learned, it is incumbent upon the coach to find or create new drills that will make the players practice the skill in a new way or under different conditions. For instance, if a player has become adept at dribbling in place, the coach may have the player dribble two basketballs in place.

In general, there should be an *offensive portion* and *defensive portion* during practice. Each portion should focus on one new fundamental. In the beginning of the season the coach will need to leave more time for the instruction of each fundamental because he will not know how quickly the players will learn. However, after time he will be able to gauge how long it will take for explanation, demonstration, correction, and repetition. Each segment should build on the previous one. For instance, if in the previous week the players learned how to dribble, then the next practice they should be able to go right into a dribbling drill to review the skill. After the drill is over the coach would then introduce a new fundamental, i.e., passing. Then he would follow the same four steps with regard to explanation, demonstration, correction, and repetition. During the next practice he would then have the players do a dribbling drill, a passing drill, and introduce a new skill. This would continue throughout the season.

Another segment that must be built into a practice is *game procedures*. For instance, if a coach has a group of kids that have never played basketball, he will have to spend time going over such things as how to substitute, lining up for a free throw, inbounding the ball, backcourt, etc. However, if players are knowledgeable in these areas then the coach must allot time to go over a particular offense or defense, or what to do against a press or possibly teach the players how to press. What is done in practice depends on the skill level of the players.

Getting Their Attention

Because coaches have a limited amount of practice time, it is important that they be able to get their players' attention quickly. The following are several ways of doing this:

- *Whistle*

Players stop whatever they are doing and get into a basketball stance near the coach whenever they hear three short blasts of the whistle. The players stand with their feet shoulder-width apart, backs nearly straight, knees and shoulders facing forward, and hands in front of their chest with their palms out. Their head should be erect and slightly forward over the feet. The players are expected to listen to all instructions given and then move quickly to follow directions. Besides getting the players' attention, this technique helps the younger kids develop a proper stance even without the basketball and trains the muscles to memorize the correct stance. Players use this stance to guard, protect the ball, dribble, pass, catch, shoot, and jump.

- *Last person*

In this technique, whenever coaches want the players to gather and listen, they call out, "last person." The players are expected to stop whatever they are doing and hustle over to stand or take a knee near the coach. The last person to arrive is penalized in a manner determined by the coach.

- *No-talk rule*

Telling the team there will be no talking for the first five minutes of practice establishes an environment that makes it easier for the coach to get the players' attention. Players who break the rule will be penalized in a manner determined by the coach.

- *Hard-conditioning drill*

Beginning practice with a drill that increases the players' heart rate and breathing is another good attention-getter. While the players are catching their breath, they are less likely to be talking among themselves. This recovery period is a good time for the coach to give instructions.

- *Soft-talk technique*

Many coaches get their players' attention by speaking in a low voice that can only be heard if everyone is quiet. Coaches who use this technique should make sure the players really have to concentrate to hear them.

Coaching Youth Basketball

Coaching youth basketball requires much more than knowledge of the X's and O's of the game. Setting up an effective practice plan requires a great deal of preparation. Working with young players involves more than simply teaching them the necessary techniques; coaches must first help them develop the necessary agility and coordination. Youth coaches should also be prepared to deal with the fragile egos and self-images of children.

Coaching youth basketball means more than winning and losing, developing skills, and creating a fun environment. It also means building relationships that exist beyond the basketball season. Youth basketball coaches create impressions that can last the rest of a player's life.

Young athletes look up to their coaches. They expect their coaches to be examples of sportsmanship, hard work, dedication, responsibility, and fairness. This responsibility is the single most important task of the youth basketball coach, but too many coaches do not take it seriously.

A Practice without a Gym

Too often coaches at every level complain about the lack of gym time to practice. Even if your program is one of the best, there will be times when your gym is unavailable due to parents' meetings, school dances, auctions, etc. When this happens, go undeterred to the cafeteria or a stage in the auditorium and move tables and chairs around until you have created enough space to conduct the following one-hour workout:

10 minutes: Stretching and loosening up

5 minutes: Jumping drills with jump ropes or small hurdles

10 minutes: Every player has a ball—work on stationary dribbling/ball handling skills

5 minutes: Two-man passing drills

5 minutes: Tipping the ball against the wall; use one hand held straight up, locked at the elbow; tip ball against the wall with a flick of the wrist. See how many consecutive tips can be made while jumping without losing the ball.

5 minutes: Triple-threat position—work on the head-and-shoulder fakes, pass/fakes, and shot fakes

5 minutes: Defensive stance and defensive slide drills

5 minutes: Have a defender guard the player with the basketball. The offensive players have to pivot and rock, protecting the ball by swinging their arms. The defenders work on staying down in the basketball position and try to distract the offensive players by placing their hand where the basketball is.

10 minutes: Form shooting—players lie on their back and shoot the ball upward. Players pair off with a partner and while sitting on chairs, shoot the ball back and forth. The emphasis should be on the correct technique and form of the elbow, wrist (cocked), the follow-through and the rotation of the basketball.

5 minutes: Conditioning—run the stairs, run outside, or run the hallways

This concludes a crisp, 65-minute workout that emphasizes the skills of the game—a workout for which you do not need a gym or a basket. You should always feel that *where there's a will, there's a way*, and pass that along to your players.

Questions Coaches Must Answer

Several questions, whether spoken or unspoken, that youth coaches owe their players answers to are as follows:

- Do you know what you are talking about?
- Can I trust you?
- Do you value me as a person, not just an athlete who plays basketball?
- Are you committed to the team?

If coaches can answer yes to all these questions, they cannot fail. Coaches are teachers, and they have a unique opportunity to influence the attitudes and character of young people. Basketball players and coaches experience a wide range of emotions: determination, anticipation, exhilaration, joy, disappointment, frustration, and bitterness. Each day presents an opportunity for players to recognize, handle, and learn from these experiences. Therefore, the coach has the responsibility of being prepared for such opportunities.

Coaches should always be concerned about the safety and welfare of each individual player. The health and well-being of the athlete should always take precedence over anything else, and coaches should always consider these factors before making decisions. This concern for a player's welfare does not end with physical well-being; the psychological health of an athlete is also crucial.

Coaches are responsible for emphasizing sportsmanship, motivation, self-discipline, loyalty, leadership, and team play to their athletes. Team sports present an opportunity for youngsters to learn to work together to accomplish goals. Coaches should encourage players to be the best they can be, but the goal of youth sports should never be to win at all costs.

Coaches should explain to all team members and their parents the importance of safety, proper care of equipment and uniforms, and team rules. It is a good idea to hold a preseason meeting that all players must attend with at least one of their parents. Coaches should inform every one of all team guidelines, particularly those regarding promptness; acceptable language and conduct; the treatment of teammates, opponents, and referees; and, with older players, the use of alcohol and drugs. Rules should be enforced fairly and consistently. When dealing with younger players, coaches should speak in terms they can understand. Good communication between coaches and players, and coaches and parents at this preseason meeting will minimize problems during the season. Youth coaches should remember parents are entrusting them with their greatest treasure: their sons and daughters.

The following are some recommendations to help coaches become the most effective coach they can be and fulfill their responsibilities to their players:

- Coaches should dress appropriately for coaching basketball. Sweatpants or shorts, an appropriate shirt, and tennis shoes or basketball shoes are essential. Coaches who do not look like coaches immediately lose the respect of their players.

- Coaches should be the first to arrive for and the last to leave a practice or game. They should also come prepared.

- Coaches should not smoke in the presence of their squad.

- Coaches should not curse or use demeaning language.

- Coaches should be as positive as possible. When they criticize, they should follow it up with a compliment. They should not embarrass their players.

- Coaches should demand respect from their players, both for themselves and for any other authority figure speaking to them.

- Coaches should build spirit by example. They should applaud good effort and hustle and single out players who make a good pass or get a tough rebound. They should praise players for improving a specific skill, and not simply look at points scored or the good players on the team.

- Coaches should not abuse or criticize the officials. When players see their coaches behave in this manner, they also begin to behave that way.

- Coaches should not make excuses for losses or poor play.

- Coaches should talk to fellow coaches. They should always be willing to listen and learn when they talk to opposing coaches or coaches whom they respect. No one knows it all. Sharing ideas with others helps people learn and grow.

- Because of their limited practice time, coaches should develop and use drills that combine various skills and are fun, easy to understand, and relatively short (10 minutes maximum).

- Coaches should be observant and correct players when they are performing techniques incorrectly.

- Coaches should have a written practice plan when they come to practice. They should get their players' attention and keep the players on task to stay on schedule.

There have been many studies regarding youth sports. According to surveys, the following are the seven most important reasons youngsters plays sports. Parents and coaches alike should notice that winning is not one of the reasons given.

- To have fun
- To improve skills
- For the excitement of competition
- To do something they are good at
- To stay in shape
- For the challenge of competition
- To be part of a team or to be with their friends

When players leave a team at the end of a season, the coach's goal should be for them to have had a great experience. Coaches should want them to always remember their time on the team as fun, challenging, and meaningful. The greatest compliment of all is when a player's parents tell the coach their child really learned important lessons about basketball and life.

Basketball Coaching Absolutes

- Basketball success is predicated on execution of fundamentals.
- The coach is the teacher. The subject is fundamentals.
- The well-conditioned team can always stay competitive.
- At lower levels winning is more related to good offense.
- Simple is better.
- Players draw confidence from their coach. The coach should always try to appear organized, alert, knowledgeable, and poised.
- Breakdown drills are essential to team success.
- Players need motivation to work on their own but at the coach's pace.

CHAPTER 10

Tips for Players

Often times a player will want to know what he can do to improve his game. This chapter covers a number of topics both physical and mental that will assist all players in their development.

Keep Moving without the Ball

Moving without the ball does two things: first, it shows the coach a desire to work and succeed; and second, a player that moves without the ball will have success long before a player who stands still.

Be the First

Be the first in line, to practice, in sprints, to hustle, to dive on the floor, and to talk.

Talk

Vocalize the action that is occurring. For instance, call, "shot," every time a shot is taken. Call out picks when they occur. Remind teammates to block-out. Call out the receiver's name when passing the ball. Always congratulate a teammate for a good play.

Treat the Ball as a Valuable Possession

A player who does not turnover the ball will play. Being able to pass, catch, and dribble while under pressure will instill confidence in any coach and will ensure playing time.

Make Lay-ups and Free Throws

Nothing will frustrate a coach more than missed scoring opportunities. Being able to make lay-ups will help the team succeed. Making free throws in or out of pressure situations will make any player more valuable to the team.

Have a Positive Attitude

Having a positive attitude will guarantee enjoyment no matter how many games are won, or how much playing time is received. Also, having a positive attitude accelerates the ability to learn and therefore accelerates success.

Look the Coach in the Eye

This shows the coach that the player cares. It also shows maturity on the listener's part. Finally, looking the coach in the eye promotes understanding and learning.

Be on Time

Being on time shows respect to the coach and to teammates. Being punctual is a good habit in any endeavor.

Play Against Older and Better Players

The best way to improve is to simply play against older and better players. While this may be frustrating at times, it will nonetheless accelerate a player's development. Also, once a player has some success against older players, it will have a tremendous effect on that player's confidence and understanding of the game when he plays against players of the same age.

Focus on Improving

A developing player's focus should be on improving. Every game and practice that the player participates in should not be evaluated on winning or losing, or how many points he scored. Instead, the player's evaluation should be based on how much he improved.

Rich Grawer was the head coach of men's basketball at Saint Louis University for 10 years. During that time he averaged 16 wins per season, and twice finished second in the NIT tournament. Grawer holds the Billiken's record for most wins in a single season with 27, and is widely credited with developing the basketball program into what it is today. Prior to becoming head coach at Saint Louis University, Grawer was an assistant coach at the University of Missouri-Columbia. During his college coaching career he coached several future NBA players, including Anthony Bonner and Steve Stipanovich. Before joining the college ranks, Grawer spent 12 years as the coach at DeSmet High School in St. Louis, posting a record of 270-87 that included three state championships and a 63-game winning streak.

Now the athletic director at Clayton High School, Grawer is in demand as a speaker and holds clinics across the nation and around the world. He and his wife, Theresa, live in St. Louis with their six children, all of whom played youth and high school basketball. Three of their children—Kevin, Brian, and Rick—received college basketball scholarships.

Sally Tippett Rains has co-authored several sports books including *Youth Baseball: A Coach's and Parent's Guide* with Wendell Kim and *Softball Pitching Fundamentals and Techniques* with Carie Dever-Boaz. She and her husband, Rob Rains, wrote *Playing on His Team*, a book about role model athletes. Her background includes working as a sports writer for KMOX Radio in St. Louis and writing several articles for *The Sporting News*.

Rains is a writing coach at Webster University in St. Louis, where she lives with husband, Rob, and her two sons, B.J. and Mike.